INTERNATIONAL DEVELOPMENT IN FOCUS

Opportunities for Environmentally Healthy, Inclusive, and Resilient Growth in Mexico's Yucatán Peninsula

Ernesto Sánchez-Triana, Jack Ruitenbeek,
Santiago Enriquez, and Katharina Siegmann, Editors

WORLD BANK GROUP

Contents

Figures

Maps

Tables

Foreword

The Yucatán Peninsula, comprising the Mexican states of Campeche, Quintana Roo, and Yucatán, is well known for its unique natural and cultural wealth. The peninsula's coastal territory extends for some 2,000 kilometers and spans the oil fields of the Gulf of Mexico to the world-renowned beaches of Cancún and Cozumel, just north of the second largest barrier reef in the world. Mayan temples, including Chichén Itzá, Ek Balám, Uxmal, and Dzibilchaltún, attest to the peninsula's cultural richness.

However, the peninsula is also a land of contrasts. Local populations, including indigenous communities, are largely absent in rapidly growing economic sectors, such as tourism. In addition, with poverty far from eliminated, and economic development opportunities beckoning in agriculture, manufacturing, and hydrocarbon development, the region faces myriad development choices, many of which carry environmental risk. Over the past decade, the peninsula has already seen environmental threats to its economic success, with challenges ranging from oil spills to hurricanes, coral bleaching, extreme flooding, and erosion.

This book discusses key sustainability challenges and identifies opportunities to address urgent problems in the Yucatan Peninsula. It lays out an agenda to set the peninsula on an environmentally healthy, inclusive, and resilient growth trajectory. Recognizing that coastal areas underpin the main economic activities of the three states on the peninsula, the book frames its discussion around an integrated coastal zone management framework. Taking advantage of the findings from robust geomorphology analysis, the book explores the potential contributions of shore management plans as a valuable coastal management tool that offers flexibility to combat widespread shoreline erosion and to better position the Yucatán Peninsula to adapt to climate change effects over the coming decades.

The book also demonstrates how rigorous economic tools can provide insights into the economic impacts of extreme climate events and of economic losses from environmental degradation. Environmental health risks in the peninsula are severe and include household air pollution in homes that still rely on wood for cooking; lead exposure; inadequate water supply, sanitation, and hygiene; and ambient air pollution in urban areas such as Cancún and Merida. Collectively, these risks result in more than 1,000 premature deaths every year and in more than 9.36 million days lost to illness just on the Peninsula alone.

In addition to pain and suffering, these risks also result in costs, including medical expenses, forgone wages, and loss of productivity. Added together, these economic losses are equivalent to 2.2–3.3 percent of the peninsula's gross income.

Extreme weather events recurrently impact the Yucatán Peninsula, often with catastrophic consequences, as evidenced by hurricanes Gilbert (1988) and Wilma (2005). Available information discussed in this book suggests that the frequency and intensity of such events will likely increase in the future as a result of climate change. The annual costs caused by these events are equivalent to about 1.5 percent of the region's gross income by 2020. A number of policy alternatives are already available to increase social and natural resilience to these events. The tourism sector illustrates how the adoption of environmentally healthy, inclusive, and resilient growth principles would simultaneously contribute to economic growth, reduced inequality, and the protection of ecosystems that can provide natural protection against growing natural hazards.

As the climate and society change in the coming years, institutions will have to evolve to deliver innovative solutions to current challenges and prepare for future events. Thus, the book also explores the potential contributions that institutional strengthening and regulatory measures can make to environmentally sustainable development that does not undermine economic growth prospects. The publication also highlights the critical role of research in filling scientific gaps in order to inform future planning.

The underlying objective of this book is to provide an interdisciplinary framework that will increase understanding of the development challenges of the Yucatán Peninsula. It aims to stimulate further discussion on how to improve the population's prospects for overcoming present and future challenges, particularly for the poor and other vulnerable groups.

Karin Kemper
Global Director
Environment, Natural Resources, and
Blue Economy Global Practice

Pablo Saavedra
Country Director
Mexico

Acknowledgments

This report is the result of the fruitful collaboration between the government of Mexico, the state governments of Campeche, Quintana Roo, and Yucatán, and The World Bank.

This book is a product of a core team that included Ernesto Sánchez-Triana (Task Team Leader), Jack Ruitenbeek, Santiago Enriquez, John Pethick, Pasquale Scandizzo, and Katharina Siegmann. The extended team included Yewande Awe, Daniele Cufari, Mayra Guerra López, Diana Gabriela Jimenez, Bjorn Larsen, Tapas Paul, Gregorio Posada, Geise Santos, John M. Skjelvick, and Elena Strukova Golub. The task team is also thankful for the support of the World Bank management team including Karin Kemper (Global Director, Environment, Natural Resources, and Blue Economy Global Practice), Valerie Hickey (Practice Manager), Pablo Saavedra (Country Director), Gerardo Corrochano (Country Director), Jutta Ursula Kern (Country Manager), and Gregor Wolf (Program Leader). Peer reviewers Dan Biller, Helena Naber, and Akiko Nakagawa provided valuable guidance. Editorial and manuscript preparation was provided by Stan Wanat.

We would like to acknowledge the valuable contributions from representatives from Mexico's Secretariat of Environment and Natural Resources, including the Under-Secretariat of Environmental Policy and Planning, the General Direction for Climate Change Policy, and the General Direction for the Federal Maritime Terrestrial Zone and Coastal Ecosystems, as well as from the National Institute of Ecology and Climate Change. We are also thankful for insightful comments provided by representatives from the Secretariat of Environment, Biodiversity and Climate Change of the government of Campeche; the Secretariat of Ecology and Environment of the government of Quintana Roo; and the Secretariat of Sustainable Development of the government of Yucatán.

We are particularly grateful to the governments of Spain and the Republic of Korea for their kind support through the Spanish Fund for Latin America and the Caribbean and the Korean Green Growth Trust Fund.

About the Contributors

Santiago Enriquez is an international consultant with 20 years of experience in the design, implementation, and evaluation of policies relating to the environment, climate change, and clean energy. He has developed analytical work for the World Bank, United States Agency for International Development, and the Inter-American Development Bank on topics that include mainstreaming of environmental and climate change considerations in key economic sectors, institutional and organizational analyses to strengthen environmental management, and policy-based strategic environmental assessments. From 1998 to 2002, he worked at the International Affairs Unit of Mexico's Ministry of Environment and Natural Resources. Enriquez holds a master's degree in public policy from the Harvard Kennedy School.

Bjorn Larsen is an international development economist and consultant to international and bilateral development agencies and research institutions with 30 years of professional experience. His primary fields of consulting and research are environmental health and natural resource management from over 50 countries in Asia, Central and South America, Europe, Middle East and North Africa, and Sub-Saharan Africa. Fields of expertise include environmental health risk assessment, health valuation, cost-benefit analysis, poverty-environment linkages, child malnutrition and environment linkages, natural resource degradation and valuation, poverty and natural resources, household survey design and administration, and statistical analysis of household survey data. He has worked extensively on household air pollution from solid fuels, urban air pollution, water supply, sanitation and hygiene, lead and arsenic exposure, and child nutrition and health.

John Pethick is an internationally renowned coastal geomorphologist with worldwide experience of coastal management stretching over half a century. His work on soft engineering as the basis of coastal management has been widely publicized and he has written extensively on this and other coastal management issues. He has developed coastal management programs based on geomorphological principals in the United Kingdom and in South Asia and Central America.

His work as consultant to the World Bank on the Sundarban of West Bengal and Bangladesh has highlighted the negative impacts of coastal defenses on low lying coastal communities and has provoked considerable worldwide interest by suggesting that defenses can actually increase risk and that retreat is often the most sustainable option.

Jack Ruitenbeek has over 35 years of experience providing policy advice in the fields of energy, natural resource, and environmental economics. His international development work has focused on advisories to the private sector, national governments, the World Bank, international nongovernmental organizations, and various bilateral development agencies, highlighting areas such as carbon and protected area finance, coastal zone management policy, and disaster risk management. Ruitenbeek holds a PhD from the London School of Economics, as well as degrees in economics and physics from the University of Calgary. He routinely provides independent expert evidence to regulatory authorities in North America and is a founding member of the Canadian Society for Ecological Economics. His current interests include planning and establishment of dark sky preserves.

Ernesto Sánchez-Triana is the Global Lead for Environmental Health and Pollution Management for the World Bank. He has worked on projects in numerous countries, including Afghanistan, Argentina, Bangladesh, Bhutan, Bolivia, Brazil, Ecuador, India, the Lao People's Democratic Republic, Mexico, Pakistan, Panama, Paraguay, and Peru. Before joining the World Bank, he worked for the Inter-American Development Bank, the Colombian Petroleum Institute, and Occidental Petroleum. He also served as Director of Environmental Policy at Colombia's National Department of Planning and as President of the Board of Directors of the Cundinamarca Environmental Protection Agency. Sánchez-Triana has led the preparation of numerous policy-based programs, investment projects, technical assistance operations, and analytical works. He holds an engineering degree from Universidad de Los Andes (Colombia), and two master's of science degrees and a PhD from Stanford University.

Pasquale Lucio Scandizzo holds a PhD from the University of California, Berkeley, and is currently Professor of Political Economy, Senior Fellow, and Board Member of the Economics Foundation at the University of Rome "Tor Vergata," Economic Adviser of the Ministry of the Economy and Finance. He is also President of the Italian Association of Development Economists and Chairman of Openeconomics, a university spinoff focusing on project evaluation and economic development. He has more than 40 years of professional experience and has developed methodologies for the economic evaluation of public projects under uncertainty using real option theory and general equilibrium techniques, leading their application in both developed and developing countries. Among many topics, his research, whose results have been widely published, concerns the relationship between institutions and economic development, with focus on risk aversion, the distribution of rights, and the demand-supply nexus in a general equilibrium framework.

Katharina Siegmann is an Environmental Specialist with the World Bank's Environment and Natural Resource Department, based in Mexico City. She joined the World Bank in 2013 and oversees the Bank's forest and REDD+ projects in Mexico, as well as forest and climate change-related projects in Central America. Siegmann holds a master's degree in international law and economics from the University of Erlangen-Nurnberg/Germany. Before joining the World Bank, she worked at the Inter-American Development Bank's Climate Change Department.

Elena Strukova Golub is an expert in environmental economics and environmental finance, specifically in cost of environmental degradation and cost-benefit analysis. She has published several peer-reviewed books and papers, and has extensive work experience in transition and developing countries in the field of environmental, energy, and climate policy including technical analysis and policy advisory role. As a World Bank consultant for more than 20 years, she was involved in the cost of environmental degradation and benefit-cost analysis studies in Latin America, South Asia, Africa, Middle East, and Eastern and Central Europe. Also, she served as the Organisation for Economic Co-operation and Development expert on environmental finance, energy subsidies elimination, natural resources, and pollution fees, and the United Nations Development Programme expert on adaptation to climate change.

Executive Summary

**ERNESTO SÁNCHEZ-TRIANA, JACK RUITENBEEK, AND
SANTIAGO ENRIQUEZ**

CONTEXT

Some 4 million people inhabit Mexico's Yucatán Peninsula within a short distance of 1,941 linear kilometers of coastline. The regional economy of the three states in the peninsula—Campeche, Yucatán, and Quintana Roo—demonstrates both the diversity of activities and the interdependence between the coast and economic growth. Quintana Roo is Mexico's second-largest tourist destination, having received some 10.8 million visitors in 2013. Mining, oil, and gas feature strongly in Campeche's economy. They are an important impetus to ongoing development and the need for coastal infrastructure. Nearly 30 percent of Mexico's fossil fuel reserves are located on the Campeche Sound and in the deep sea of the Gulf of Mexico. The state of Yucatán similarly depends on natural and cultural tourism; in 2012, the state's main archeological sites (Chichén Itzá, Ek Balám, Uxmal, and Dzibilchaltún) received 2.15 million visitors.

For the three states of the Yucatán Peninsula, coastal areas underpin the main economic activities. The region faces potentially major impacts due to population growth, infrastructure development, and economic activity. However, the state of environmental management in the peninsula has not kept up with this level of economic activity, both in terms of knowledge production and of regulation. As a result, coastal and marine ecosystems have suffered.

Climate change could also have significant impacts on the Yucatán Peninsula, including an increase in the frequency and intensity of extreme weather events and alteration of marine ecosystems (for example, coral bleaching). Because of its vulnerability to hurricanes, floods, and sea level rise, the Yucatán Peninsula is expected to become much more vulnerable to climate events (map ES.1). The Yucatán Peninsula is anticipated to experience the largest increases in temperature in Mexico, and climate change could potentially increase the poverty rate from 15.13 percent to 18.81 percent by 2030.

In response to this challenge, the state governments from the Yucatán Peninsula requested World Bank support to strengthen the knowledge to support coastal management, as well as to leverage the region's natural capital to support an economic development that is socially inclusive, clean,

MAP ES.1

Tracks of hurricanes, tropical storms, and tropical depressions that hit Yucatán, 1970–2014

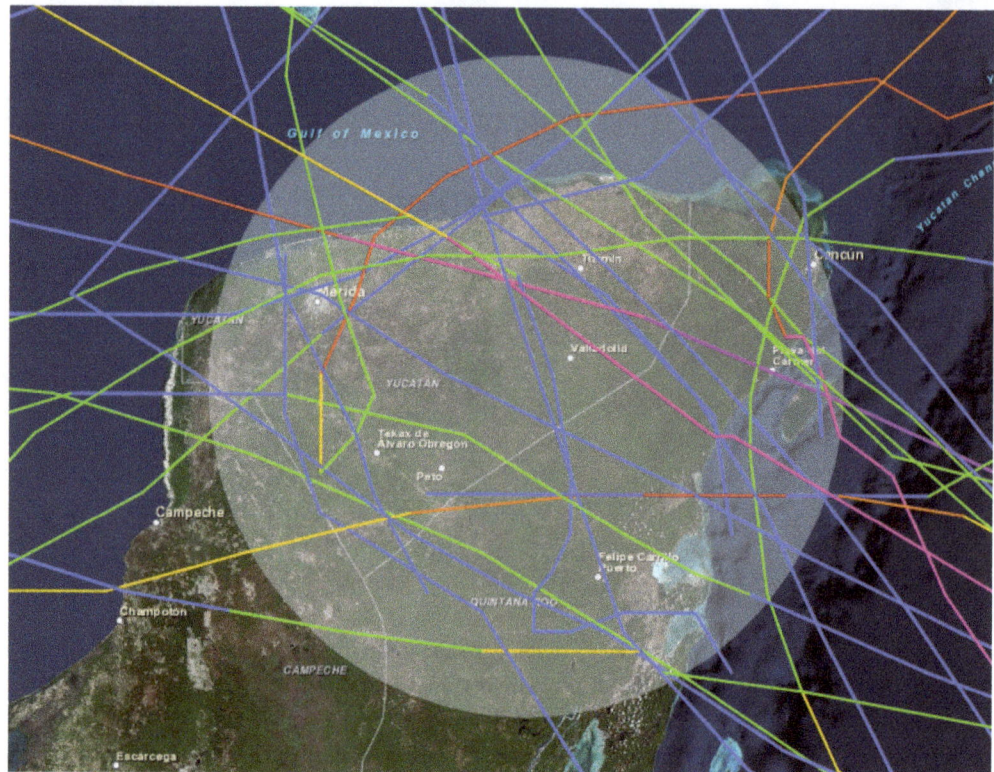

Source: NOAA 2016a.
Note: Green = tropical storm; Blue = tropical depression; Yellow = hurricane category 1 (sustained winds of 119–153 km/h); Orange = hurricane category 2 (sustained winds of 154–177 km/h); Red = hurricane category 3 (sustained winds of 178–208 km/h); Pink = hurricane category 4 (sustained winds of 209–251 km/h).

efficient, and resilient. In response to this request, the World Bank conducted analytical work and engaged a wide stakeholder base to identify priority issues, assess alternative policies, and lay the foundation to continuously bolster knowledge generation and management in these areas.

An interdisciplinary team conducted the analytical work summarized in this report. Economic analysis was used to quantify and prioritize the costs of environmental degradation and natural disasters, which have among the highest impacts on the Yucatán Peninsula. A different type of economic analysis was used to develop a Social Accounting Matrix (SAM) representing the flows of all economic transactions that take place within the Quintana Roo economy. The SAM helped to provide quantitative estimates on the environmental sustainability, economic contributions, and social implications of alternative tourism development scenarios in Quintana Roo. Geomorphological studies helped to assess challenges and opportunities for coastal management in the Yucatán Peninsula, with a view towards addressing current erosion problems and anticipated climate change impacts, such as sea level rise. Policy and institutional analysis underpinned the recommendations presented within this report.

A number of institutions participated in discussions and workshops with the team that conducted the analytical work. These included federal organizations, particularly Mexico's Secretariat of Environment and Natural Resources (SEMARNAT) and the National Institute of Ecology and Climate Change (INECC).

At the state level, representatives from Campeche's Secretariat of Environment and Sustainable Use (SMAAS), Quintana Roo's Secretariat of Ecology and Environment (SEMA), and Yucatán's Secretariat of Urban Development and Environment (SEDUMA) provided leadership and guidance. Academic researchers and representatives from Civil Society Organizations from the Yucatán Peninsula also provided valuable insights and shared ongoing efforts.

INTEGRATED COASTAL ZONE MANAGEMENT AND ITS ROLE IN ENVIRONMENTALLY HEALTHY, RESILIENT, AND INCLUSIVE GROWTH

Habitation in coastal areas is common and people have been dealing with changes in coastal systems since time immemorial. Adaptation to change is nothing new in human history. However, integrated coastal zone management (ICZM) has become more frequently adopted as a formal, semi-codified process that attempts to reconcile conflicts and capture opportunities among stakeholders and traditional economic sectors in the coastal zone and marine areas. Key precepts of ICZM generally include (a) an initial assessment of conditions based on best available science, (b) risk assessments, (c) formulation of cost-effective interventions, (d) implementation of priority interventions through a wide range of stakeholders, and (e) continuous monitoring and evaluation within a long-term process that permits updates in knowledge and adaptation through new or reformed interventions. Its scope also permits a broader form of objectives encompassing social well-being and environmental sustainability in addition to traditional economic growth. In complex systems such as the coastal resources of the Yucatán Peninsula, ICZM thus provides an approach for achieving economic growth that respects environmental constraints while promoting social and economic welfare. Recent practical ICZM approaches have also focused on the *reduction of vulnerability* under uncertainty, and the incorporation of ideas of the *global commons* in the integration of global fishery issues, greenhouse gas (GHG) emission reduction, and other issues that extend beyond a simple coastal stretch.

ICZM is a potentially demanding process that requires adequate information and strong institutions. It calls for focusing efforts on targeted issues and improving the information base on which decisions are made. Many Latin American governments have instituted sectoral approaches to environmental development: individual laws and procedures for measuring and mitigating environmental impacts in individual sectors (tourism, mining, agricultural, and so forth). However, these laws lead to an ad hoc approach and fail to capture the cumulative impacts of all associated activities. Nonetheless, in terms of drawing lessons from ICZM, in many cases it is "too early to tell." By its nature, ICZM is an intergenerational undertaking. Many regard some of the early experiences in the United States and Europe to be successful, but there too, more-recent advances in coastal management have seen the promotion of managed retreat or realignment of shorelines. This process abandons decades, or even centuries, of efforts to use hard defenses as a management mechanism. However, even such backtracking can be interpreted as a success; it shows that decision making adapts as new information becomes available.

Few countries have the formal regulatory structures that permit comprehensive management of large spaces and sensitive ecosystems in an integrated manner. In Mexico, command-and-control regulations based on a sectoral approach exist, as do other piecework environmental regulations, but there is no structure to tie together various jurisdictions and ministries and coordinate their actions, let alone coordinate among different sectors for ICZM. However, concerning the regulatory framework, something approaching ICZM is undertaken in Mexico largely through three policy instruments: (a) Environmental Impact Assessment (EIA), (b) the creation of Marine Protected Zones, and (c) Ecological Zoning.

In Mexico, there are significant capacity and regulatory gaps that hinder the implementation of EIA in general and, in particular, for cumulative impacts. EIA practice in Mexico has a number of limitations, including inadequate scoping, elaboration of environmental impact studies based on incomplete data, insufficient participation from external experts in the preparation and evaluation of environmental impact statements, faulty public participation, absence of clear criteria to evaluate environmental impact statements, and weak enforcement and follow-up to ensure that the project developer complies with all the requirements that SEMARNAT established during the EIA process. In brief, Mexico's EIA system in its current form is not well suited for coastal zone management.

Mexico has 177 Natural Protected Areas, of which nearly 70 span over marine or coastal ecosystems. There has been debate over how to use these marine protected areas (MPAs) as an avenue for ICZM, particularly in the Gulf of Mexico. Indeed, ecological processes within the Gulf's marine environment cannot be separated from those that occur along the coast and within the river systems. Everything is connected, but no overall plan for managing the health of the gulf currently exists. A challenge is to integrate coastal zone management with Large Marine Ecosystems (LME) management, and to develop plans that take into account the health of the entire gulf.

Mexico's Ecological Zoning Program is more promising as a means for putting ICZM into action. Through a consultative process, stakeholders can agree upon a set of requirements for development in a given ecological area. All subsequent projects are then required, through the EIA regulation, to adhere to these requirements. Territorial Environmental Land Use Programs (*Programas de Ordenamiento Ecológico General del Territorio* or POEGTs) are regional development plans developed through participatory processes in which local, state, and federal government stakeholders, as well as civil society and academics, come together in a process designed to maximize consensus. These instruments have been extensively used in Mexico, including throughout the Yucatán Peninsula, but results have been inconclusive. To date, there have been no rigorous attempts to evaluate the effectiveness and efficiency of the preparation and enforcement of POEGTs, most of which lack an appropriate monitoring and evaluation framework. In fact, most of Mexico's coastal zones lack a POEGT. However, these plans are a valuable consensus-making tool and provide one of the best ways of formalizing the necessary agreements if various municipalities, states, and ministries are going to work together.

As described previously, adaptation to change is a natural human response. Climate change adaptation (CCA) can be documented back to the ice age. One potential way forward is to link ICZM efforts to ongoing CCA efforts. Mexico has been proactive in addressing climate change. The country's mitigation strategy is one of the strongest and most developed among middle- and low-income countries. In terms of adaptation, the country is still in the planning stages: addressing capacity and designing interventions. Under the climate change law, Mexico intends to alter patterns of development with a view to limiting vulnerability.

The law would also conserve ecosystems to retain natural barriers to cyclonic storms and other climate events. For instance, in Quintana Roo, authorities are taking proactive steps, through a cross-cutting Office of Climate Change, to enact policies for altering land use in coastal areas and for mitigating disaster risk. In many cases, the practices undertaken as part of climate change initiatives—particularly the changes in land use—are similar to those that would be undertaken through ICZM. However, efforts are hampered by the difficulty of managing participatory processes, by the distribution of responsibilities among many different agencies, and by the lack of specific funding allocated to CCA. A first step has been taken to overcome those hurdles by the creation of the regional climate change commission for the Yucatán Peninsula, a joint committee created by the three states that seeks to coordinate efforts on climate change mitigation and adaptation. The commission still faces several challenges, including lack of a solid jurisdictional mandate and institutionalization, absence of funding for the institution itself, and limited availability of funds for specific interventions.

COASTAL GEOMORPHOLOGY AND THE ROLE OF SHORELINE MANAGEMENT PLANS

The entire coastal zone of the peninsula is one of outstanding natural resources and beauty, which has enabled its tourism industry to become a significant sector of Mexico's economy. Most of the tourist industry is focused on the coastal zone and its coastal reefs, shoreline beaches, and ecologically important lagoons. The Biosphere Reserves of Sian Ka'an in Quintana Roo, Ría Celestún in Yucatán, and Laguna de Términos in Campeche reflect the national and international importance of the coastal ecology of the Yucatán Peninsula. They also provide a range of habitats that is dependent upon its physical characteristics—a karstic platform with few rivers, low tidal range, and a series of barrier islands. However, these natural resources face increasing threats from external changes such as increases in sea level and hurricane frequency, and from the presence of coastal infrastructure and its associated extensive and uncoordinated coastal defenses.

Sea level rise, both existing and predicted, is likely to be the major factor affecting Yucatán coastal behavior over the next few decades. Landward migration of the barrier beaches due to existing sea level rise, exacerbated by accelerated eustatic sea level rise and local seasonal fluctuations, both due to global warming, will affect all shoreline properties. Sand inundation of backshore properties will also occur as barriers roll over. Shore defenses to combat the erosion, already deployed by local residents, will lead to increased erosion down drift.

A preliminary examination of the tide gauge records from Progreso and Ciudad de Carmen, undertaken for this study, suggests a relative sea level rise over the past few decades of between 3 and 5 mm per year. This existing rise in sea level may be in addition to that predicted to occur because of global warming. Current IPCC predictions under a low emission scenario (that is, RCP 2.6) are for a total rise in sea level of 0.26 m by 2100 and 0.95 m for a worst-case scenario (that is, RCP 8.5). However, many authorities consider that this underestimates the threat and suggest that eustatic sea level will rise by between 0.5 and 2.0 m. This, together with the existing rate of 3–5 mm per year on the Yucatán coast, would mean a total sea level rise of between 0.77 m and 2.45 m by the end of the century. In addition, the predicted rise in ocean temperatures due to global warming may increase the existing seasonal fluctuation in water levels along this coast.

Coastal erosion

Coastal erosion is now seen as a major issue for the social and economic development of all three coastal states on the Yucatán Peninsula. Rates of erosion vary according to the area under review. For example, Meyer-Arendt (1991) reports rates of 0.6 m per year at Progreso, while Gonzalez-Leija et al. (2013) reported 15 m per year at Cancún. In contrast, Diez (2009), working on the Cancún shore, reports a 34 m retreat in the period 1984–2004, a rate of 1.7 m per year. Gutierrez-Estrada, Castro-Del Rio, and Galaviz-Solis (1988) calculated an average erosion rate 1.8 m per year for the north Yucatán coast over a 110-year period. It is important to recognize that most of the erosion records provided in the literature are for periods commencing at least 50 years ago, and in some case 100 years ago, indicating that shore erosion on the Yucatán is not a recent phenomenon.

The explanations often advanced for this widespread erosion are (a) sea level rise due to global warming, and (b) human interference in the coastal system. Neither of them provides an adequate reason for the observed erosion rates. Reported erosion rates commencing at least 100 years ago support the conclusion that the process began before extensive human development of this coast.

The most common response to coastal erosion on the Yucatán Peninsula, as elsewhere in the world, is to construct hard defenses in the form of groins and seawalls. These are intended to stave off erosion and protect from catastrophic events such as hurricanes. In Cancún, following Hurricane Gilbert in 1988, extensive repair of damaged frontage hotels and business properties took place. Defenses, mainly in the form of sea walls, but including riprap barriers, were constructed, but loss of beach material continued. This prompted a beach nourishment program, which is a second approach to addressing erosion and appears to be the presently favored means of coastal defense. Programs recently implemented or currently in progress include the 3 million cubic meter recharge at Cancún, recirculation of dredged sediment from navigation channels along the north Yucatán coast, and a proposed recharge of beaches protected by an artificial reef for a new hotel complex at San Miguelito, Quintana Roo. However, beach nourishment also depends on sediment recharge, which requires careful consideration of the sediment transport pathways prior to sediment extraction. In many cases, no such analysis is provided, leading to progressive deterioration of the coastal system.

Some insights from geomorphology

The geomorphology of the coast of the Yucatán Peninsula has not received detailed attention in the scientific literature. Several papers and books deal with the geology of the area and there is a substantial literature on the ecology of the coast; only a few authors have focused on the local dynamics of sediment and coastal morphology. There are no published accounts of the large-scale geomorphology of the peninsula. One problem facing any such investigation is the lack of primary data on coastal energy and materials. There are no wave data for the area and only two tide gauges: Progreso and Carmen. Studies of beach sediment are restricted to granulometry and chemistry, and there have been no attempts to identify beach-sand sources or sinks. However, preliminary analytical work conducted for this study has permitted some insights to be drawn of relevance to future planning:

- In southern Campeche, there are several examples where it is clear that direct human intervention has resulted in local erosion. One example of this is the erosion of the foreshore of Isla del Carmen
- In northern Campeche, the area is characterized by fine-grained sediment, and planning processes cannot be approached in the same way as those cells formed in sand-sized material. This section of the coast is undeveloped and is of high ecological value
- In Yucatán to northern Quintana Roo, preliminary observations of satellite imagery suggest that a continuous sediment pathway, identified on satellite imagery by major sand waves, exists between Isla Contoy in Quintana Roo and Celestún in Yucatán. These waves along the entire coastal zone of Yucatán and the accretion at Celestún, suggest that there is no sediment deficit on this coast. Erosion rates observed along this coast cannot necessarily be explained by changes in environmental conditions and it may be therefore that the observed erosion is due to human interference in the sediment transport pathways. An alternative explanation remains that sediment transport along this coast has gradually declined over the Holocene and that, more recently, this decline has resulted in a negative sediment budget in which potential sediment transport is not met by supply, resulting in erosion of the foreshore. These alternative hypotheses are clearly incompatible, the one suggesting a positive sediment budget and only human induced local erosion, the other proposing a long-term decline in sediment supply terminating in a negative budget today. The next planning stage should be the acquisition of a detailed database that will allow rigorous testing of such behavioral models and thus to inform the management process
- Quintana Roo is likely dominated by two sediment cells. North of Cancún, the net sediment transport pathway will be northward. South of Cancún, the pathway will be southward. A divergent sediment boundary implies either that sediment is input to the divide from offshore, or that sediment is eroded from the shore to feed the opposing sediment pathways. In this case, both the options may apply: there exists a sediment store in the straits between Isla Mujeres/Contoy and the mainland, and several authors have documented the erosion of the shoreline along the Cancún shore.

Shoreline management

To overcome the challenges of erosion requires a fundamental understanding of the processes acting on the shoreline system, and on how the system itself responds to such processes. Shoreline Management is the physical management of the shore to reduce the impact of natural hazards, such as flooding and erosion, but also to mitigate the physical impact of human intervention in the coastal system. Its overall objective is for a shore system that is self-sustaining—one that is resilient and does not require human maintenance. Shoreline management therefore constitutes one component of the larger program of ICZM; it may be thought of as providing an interface between coastal science and coastal management. The process of shoreline management includes production of a Shoreline Management Plan (SMP), designed to evaluate the behavior of a coast, both in response to environmental and human impacts, and to use this information to inform the economic, social and environmental plans for the coast. In this sense, the SMP offers information to the ICZM planners; thus, it must aim for efficient communication of relevant coastal science to ICZM planners.

A SMP sets out how the coast should best be managed in the future. It is

- An account of the past and predicted future behavior of a stretch of coastline, normally defined as a sediment cell
- A large scale assessment of the risks for people and property associated with coastal processes within the SMP area
- Designed to inform a policy framework that sustainably reduces risks to people and to the developed, historic, and natural environments—a policy framework that is central to the ICZM process.

SMPs set out the approach to achieve long-term sustainability of coastal risk management for a specific stretch of coast. Their aim is to provide the basis for sustainable shoreline management policies over the next 100 years within a natural process unit (sediment cell or sub-cell). The stretch of coast that an SMP covers includes one or more sediment cells and will typically include a number of communities and land uses, and a series of different physical features and coastal defenses.

The process of SMP development includes five main tasks:

1) Definition of sediment cells as the basic unit for coastal zone management
2) Collation of a coastal database designed to support the science within the SMP
3) Development of conceptual (or behavioral) models for each sediment cell
4) Evaluation of societal demands on the coast and
5) Reconciliation of scientific and societal demands within the SMP framework.

Table ES.1 shows the content of the final SMP. It includes a description of the physical processes of the coast, a review of its present and anticipated land use, and an outline of policies that could result in long-term sustainable use. Finally, after consultation with coastal user groups, the SMP should report on a preferred option for shoreline management that reconciles both its natural processes and the human uses.

TABLE ES.1 Structure of the shoreline management plan

SECTION	CONTENT
Coastal behavior	Outline of hindcast and forecast geomorphological behavior models of the coast within each sediment cell boundary
Prediction of future coastal behavior	Prediction of future change in large-scale morphology, flooding, and erosion risks; normally for the next 100 years
Land use	Outline of existing coastal-zone usage: agriculture, urban, ports, industry, ecological, heritage, and so forth
Coastal management objectives	Summary of known objectives for the coastal zone (development of tourism, ports, industry, urbanization, and so forth)
Policy development	Outline of policies that would allow long-term sustainable development of the coast. A series of policy units may be defined along the coast within which each policy may be applied. These may not necessarily coincide with the sediment cell boundaries. Policies may include coastal defense provision, managed retreat from coastal hazard zones, or zero development
Preferred policy selection	Selection of preferred policy for each policy unit based on economic, social, technical, and environmental criteria

The Yucatán Peninsula database

A key component of the development of an SMP should be the collection, storage, and retrieval of coastal data that can be used to develop the conceptual models of the coast. Data should be acquired from both primary and secondary (that is, existing) sources, with a bias towards secondary data to reduce both costs and time.

However, in many cases secondary data sources are either lacking or inadequate. The existing database for the Yucatán Peninsula is not considered adequate to support any detailed shoreline management. The limited available data are focused on local issues at scales significantly smaller than those of the sediment cells outlined above. This means that management tends to rely on reducing local impacts rather than seeking general causes of coastal problems. The lack of any data on waves, tides, currents, bathymetry, shoreline topography, and the minimal data on sea level rise must be seen as a major impediment to effective shoreline management. Urgent attention must be given to redress this situation.

ECONOMICS OF ENVIRONMENTAL PRIORITIES

Cost of natural disasters and climate change implications

A preliminary analysis was conducted on the data on floods, storms, and rains that are associated with the wet air masses that moved over the Atlantic and hit the Yucatán Peninsula. This analysis shows an increase in the frequency of extreme weather events, as well as growing damages per event. These trends could be largely attributed to an increase in land and water temperature in the region, which has been linked to climate change. If global temperatures were to continue this upward trend, temperatures in the region would also continue to rise and would likely be associated with an increase in the frequency and severity of extreme weather events. Table ES.2 provides a summary of projections of future temperature change and other climate change indicators for the State of Yucatán. These projections are used as a basis for demonstrating the potential economic damages from natural disasters arising from climate change.

Projections from the DICE 2009 model (Nordhaus 2010) were applied to compute an increase of global temperature from pre-industrial level up to 2050. For this analysis, the "optimal CO_2 emission scenario" from the DICE 2009 model was used. Results of DICE 2009 are consistent with the range for temperature change presented in ES.2. The analysis was thus conducted using global

TABLE ES.2 Summary of projections of future temperature change and other projected indicators of climate change for Yucatán

INDICATOR	2020	2050	2080
Temperature increase in C°	0.5–0.8	0.5–1.8	0.6–2.8
Variation of annual precipitation (%)	(−14.9%)–1%	(−14.9%)–1%	(−14.9%)–1%
Number of extremely hot days/year	7–12	9–51	10–78
Number of extremely cold days/year	19–8	26–8	33–9
Annual reduction of extremely wet days	0–13	0–13	0–13
Annual increase of extremely dry days	(−4)–16	(−4)–16	(−4)–16

Source: Government of Yucatán 2012.

temperature as the major exogenous parameter and presenting frequency and severity of extreme weather events as a function of global temperature increase.

The deadliest historical natural disasters in Yucatán took place in 1990. Overall mortality trends have remained relatively constant for the last 40 years in Mexico, but mortality from extreme weather events has fallen slightly, to the credit of official efforts to improve preparedness to these events. However, despite these efforts, the number of people affected by extreme events has increased significantly over the last 20 years.

The economic analysis relies on a per case cost for the worst disasters, looking individually at (a) lives lost, (b) people affected, (c) houses destroyed, (d) houses affected, (e) schools affected, (f) medical centers affected, (g) hectares of crop loss, and (h) livestock lost. The unit losses were translated into future potential economic losses through Monte Carlo analyses simulations driven by different climate scenarios. If gross domestic product (GDP) were to grow 2–3 percent annually in the three states in the Yucatán Peninsula, the annual mean economic cost of extreme weather events (ordinary events) would be about 0.4 percent of GDP. This figure is about twice more than the annual cost of natural disasters for Mexico as a whole. However, in the 95th percentile (when the damages would be highest) this cost could reach 1.4–1.5 percent of GDP in 2020 and 1.6–2.3 percent of GDP in 2050.

These results provide an economic valuation of potential damages from meteorological events associated with climate change. The estimates are based on economic valuation methods associated with probabilistic events. The uncertainty in cost estimates remains significant and may differ considerably depending also on the geographical incidence and timing of the event. Economic valuation of potential damages demonstrates that there is a trend of ever-increasing cost impacts. Avoiding even a small portion of such costs through appropriate emergency preparedness, risk mitigation, or similar programs would be money well spent. ICZM efforts that reduce vulnerability to these significant hazards are an important adaptation mechanism. These efforts should consider both relatively infrequent but catastrophic events, as well as events with less severe impacts but that occur frequently.

The exercise demonstrates that economic valuation can be helpful in communicating risks and in identifying priorities. In the overall ICZM context, such valuations can also be conducted to determine the economic impacts of other hazards (such as water pollution, air pollution, and soil contamination), which may be hypothesized to be relevant in specific local circumstances. Before this report, no such analyses have been undertaken for the Yucatán Peninsula; the following section summarizes another such example.

Cost of environmental degradation in the Yucatán Peninsula

In the Yucatán Peninsula, as practically everywhere else, government agencies have limited resources to develop policies and support interventions that will contribute to sustainable development. Having a rigorous methodology to set priorities is therefore essential to ensure that scarce public resources target the environmental issues that cause the most severe social and economic impacts, and particularly those that affect primarily the poor and other vulnerable groups. A methodologically rigorous approximation to identify environmental priorities is to quantify the impacts and economic costs of these issues. As part of this analysis, economic valuation techniques were used to estimate the cost of environmental degradation impacts on human health, and thus on economic and social development and well-being. To estimate these impacts, the first part of the analysis calculated the number of deaths and cases of illnesses caused by environmental problems with well-established health effects, particularly household (indoor) air pollution, outdoor air pollution, lead exposure, and inadequate water supply, sanitation, and hygiene. These calculations relied on available data at the state and national levels, as well as from an extensive literature review. Where possible and relevant, risks were estimated based on the specific characteristics of stakeholders, such as age group, or urban vs. rural settings, among others. For example, because indoor air pollution occurs within home dwellings, its impacts for different households can be more easily evaluated. Other categories of environmental degradation—such as outdoor air pollution or exposure to lead—occur in areas where the differentiation of effects across different stakeholder groups cannot be measured using the available resources and data.

After estimating the health impacts of the environmental risks, the analysis quantified the economic losses that they represent. These losses come in many forms, including loss of income, productivity, and contributions to household activities due to premature mortality, illness, and neuropsychological impairments (IQ losses). Illness also involves cost of medical treatment. These costs were quantified in monetary terms by means of valuation techniques used in economics.

Using conservative assumptions, the analysis estimates that 1,073–1,100 people died in the Yucatán Peninsula in 2013 from environmental health risks (table ES.3). In terms of health impacts in the peninsula, household air pollution is the most severe problem, followed by outdoor air pollution; these two types of air pollution are responsible for around 80 percent of deaths associated with an environmental health risk. Adult lead (Pb) exposure and inadequate water, sanitation, and hygiene caused 13 percent and 7 percent of total deaths, respectively.

From an economic standpoint, the annual cost of the environmental health effects is estimated in the range of Mex\$10,900–16,100 million in 2013, with a midpoint estimate of Mex\$13,500 million. This cost is equivalent to 2.2–3.3 percent of the Yucatán Peninsula's estimated gross regional income in 2013, with a midpoint estimate of 2.75 percent. Lead exposure is responsible for 48 percent of this cost, mostly because it results in impaired intelligence in children and a consequent reduction in lifetime earnings. About 26 percent of the cost is from household air pollution, 16 percent is from outdoor air pollution, and 10 percent of the cost is from inadequate water, sanitation and hygiene.

TABLE ES.3 **Annual deaths and days of illness from environmental risk factors in the Yucatán Peninsula, 2013**

	DEATHS			DAYS OF ILLNESS (000)		
	LOW	MID	HIGH	LOW	MID	HIGH
Lead (Pb) exposure—adults	138	138	138	337	505	674
Household air pollution	524	538	551	2,065	3,204	4,343
Outdoor air pollution	332	332	332	812	1,219	1,625
Water, sanitation, hygiene	79	79	79	3,748	4,287	4,909
Total	**1,073**	**1,087**	**1,100**	**7,049**	**9,357**	**11,747**

Source: Larsen and Skjelvik 2015.
Note: Additional impacts of lead exposure are 87–197 thousand lost IQ points per year among children under five years of age.

The analysis thus indicates that levels of exposure to environmental health risks in the Yucatán Peninsula are significant and result in a major loss of economic opportunities and quality of life, particularly for lower income groups, such as households that still use biomass fuels. To address these challenges, the state governments of the Yucatán Peninsula could consider filling additional knowledge gaps and assessing interventions targeting environmental priority problems.

Although blood lead levels have been decreasing over time, efforts should be made to identify and control lead exposure in *hotspots*. In addition, in light of recent evidence of the severity of impacts of lead in children, measurement studies should be undertaken to confirm blood lead levels among children, map geographic pockets of high blood lead levels, and identify and control sources of lead exposure.

Given the significant health effects and high cost of household use of solid fuels for cooking, increased emphasis should be placed on improved cooking stoves, ventilation, and switching of fuel to LPG. When tackling both indoor and outdoor air pollution, governmental efforts should prioritize mitigating emissions and reducing concentration of PM2.5, which is the air pollutant with the largest health effects.

Finally, improvements should be continued in the water and sanitation sector, with emphasis on bridging the sanitation gap, ensuring good quality drinking water, and continuing efforts to improve handwashing practices and other hygiene dimensions.

Although the three state governments of the Yucatán Peninsula have begun to address shared challenges jointly, notably in the case of climate change, there is currently no priority-setting mechanism in the region and the scarce available resources are not used to address the categories of environmental degradation that are causing the most significant effects. This economic analysis of health costs provides an urgently needed framework to align resources and efforts to achieve better environmental conditions. The methodologies and approach adopted by this analytical work can be replicated in the future to evaluate progress in reducing environmental conditions, identifying policy and intervention improvements, and determining the most efficient use of scarce resources. In doing so, it is crucial to continuously incorporate new scientific findings, evolving methodologies, and broader stakeholder perspectives.

Tourism and social inclusion

Another priority challenge for the Yucatán Peninsula's coastal areas is the lack of sustainability of the tourism model that has driven economic growth, particularly in Quintana Roo. This represents an important case of an economy whose development has been led by the expansion of the tourist industry organized around the traditional model of the tourist enclave and beach resort concentration. Deteriorating environmental conditions and changing international trends combined with climate change threats have made this tradition obsolete as a model of industrial organization, and increasingly unreliable as an engine of sustainable development. Moreover, the model has excluded local populations, particularly indigenous households, from its economic benefits.

Because of its riches in terms of natural beauty, cultural heritage and human potential, Quintana Roo appears particularly apt to accept the challenge of converting its economy toward the new type of tourism, based on lower scale development, devoted to the ecological and cultural aspects of the visitors' experience, higher social and economic inclusion, and a more integrated economic structure. The SAM developed as part of the analytical work helped to explore and test these hypotheses using available statistics and the results of two field surveys conducted on a sample of international and national tourists and of local households, respectively.

The analysis conducted seems to corroborate the hypothesis that Quintana Roo can develop its economy at a faster pace and with a more balanced growth by differentiating its development model through the following five sets of actions: (a) rebalance the spatial pattern of development through land use planning and regulation, with special attention to the control of urban sprawl and conservation of the coastal ecosystem; (b) promote smallscale development of the tourism supply chain more widely, based on local entrepreneurship and small and specialized operators; (c) invest in environmental and biodiversity conservation; (d) invest in tourism development through basic infrastructure (water, sanitation, and feeder roads) and non-basic infrastructure (access and maintenance of archaeological sites, parks, and museums), not only in proximity to beaches and seafronts, but also in forest and wetland areas; and (e) encourage the involvement of the indigenous population in the various segments of the tourism supply chain, including agriculture, transportation, lodging, and tourism operations.

ENVIRONMENTAL IMPACT ASSESSMENT REVISITED

Mexico's legal framework and practice are not suited to support coastal environmental management. Arguably, from its conception, EIA was not meant to be the predominant environmental management tool, but to complement other legal, economic, and administrative instruments by opening up environmental authorities' decision making to public scrutiny, particularly in relation to projects likely to cause significant environmental impacts. However, in Mexico, as in other countries, EIA has become the main environmental management tool and is often the only instrument used to address complex environmental problems, as exemplified by coastal zone management in Campeche.

In the cases reviewed for this report, EIA practice had a number of limitations. These included inadequate scoping, and elaboration of environmental impact studies based on incomplete data; insufficient participation from experts in the preparation and evaluation of the Environmental Impact Statement (MIA—"Manifestación de Impacto Ambiental"); scarce public participation; ambiguous criteria to evaluate the MIA; and weak enforcement and follow-up to ensure that the project developer complies with all the requirements that SEMARNAT established during the EIA process.

Part of the difficulties impeding better use of EIA stems from the existing legal framework. On one hand, the laws and regulations include a large number of activities for which an EIA must be undertaken. On the other hand, SEMARNAT is required to approve all MIAs, unless they fall under the specific circumstances mentioned above. As a result, SEMARNAT receives a very large number of MIAs every year, which it has to evaluate under tight deadlines. As a rough comparison, in Mexico an average of 2,786 projects per year were submitted to the EIA process between 2008 and 2012, compared with an average of 463 projects per year in the United States. The resources and time that SEMARNAT has available for each of these projects is limited, curtailing opportunities to engage other agencies, external specialists, or the public. Lack of resources is also a constraint to conduct field visits for supervision and enforcement.

As in Mexico, most countries in Latin America use lists to determine which projects or activities are subject to an EIA. The existence of such lists is supposed to reduce discretionary decision making. However, they generate a different problem: the rigidity of the lists limits their ability to filter out the actions that would not generate significant environmental effects. Lists are also used to determine whether a regional or a specific MIA should be prepared. In the specific case of coastal areas, only large aquaculture projects would call for a regional MIA. Other cases that would trigger the preparation of a regional MIA include projects with potential synergistic, cumulative, or residual impacts on ecosystems. However, there is a dearth of methodologies, guidelines, and regulations for guiding effective cumulative and synergistic impact assessments. Arguably, many projects in coastal areas would likely have cumulative or synergistic impacts. However, as the reviewed cases show, the EIA for projects in the coast of Campeche did not need to address these types of impacts.

EIA's potential contributions to ICZM are also limited because of insufficient involvement of independent experts, which is not required under the regulatory framework in place. In addition, project developers are responsible for hiring the consultant who prepares the EIA, resulting in a clear conflict of interests. Developers' main interests are meeting the bare minimum legal requirements and overcoming any potential objections to the project. Consultants thus have incentives to focus on these objectives, rather than on conducting rigorous environmental studies.

Public participation can add value to the EIA process by making visible the problems, constraints, opportunities, and challenges that tended to be hidden by limited screening, scoping, and preparation stages for the environmental impact study. However, public hearings are often resource-intensive and, if not properly organized, can easily turn into a community's opportunity to voice demands for issues with little or no relationship to the environmental impact of a project. Clearly regulating the public hearings process, as well as complying with other provisions aiming to facilitate public participation, such as ensuring that the relevant information is publicly available, could strengthen EIA practice in Mexico.

One of the fundamental contributions of EIA is the identification of mitigation measures that can be implemented to avoid, minimize, or offset the negative effects associated with the proposed project. For this reason, the EIA process includes a follow-up mechanism that would ideally help authorities to ensure that the conditions for approval are fulfilled, to monitor whether the action's environmental impacts are similar to those predicted by the environmental impact study, to assess whether the selected mitigation measures are effective, and to generate information to improve other EIAs.

In Mexico, as in other countries, environmental authorities rarely monitor the action's impacts after the corresponding license or permit has been issued, mainly due to lack of resources. Exploring mechanisms to increase the resources available to environmental agencies, such as including the cost of supervision in the fees paid by developers, is therefore crucial to improve EIA's effectiveness.

In the context of ICZM, the complexity of problems and issues does not always lend itself to a single approach. Indeed, systems that rely primarily on EIA would benefit from complementary market-based approaches, legal relief through publicly accessible regulatory and court processes, and voluntary mechanisms by industries that meet local social and environmental goals while also contributing to cost-effective operations. An appropriate way forward for EIA reforms is to identify and implement such complementary market-based approaches.

This report reviewed a range of such incentives, including (a) user charges and taxes/subsidies; (b) market creation through tradable permits and deposit/refund mechanisms; (c) market creation through payment for ecosystem services; (d) final demand intervention such as eco-labeling, disclosure requirements, and environmental awareness building; (e) final demand intervention related to supply-chain management; and (f) introduction of liability legislation that is more comprehensive. While all such approaches have their advantages and disadvantages, coastal systems and the activities within them are adequately diverse that the use of such instruments may usefully complement the currently dominant command-and-control approach.

RECOMMENDATIONS: A WAY FORWARD

This report has highlighted the need to fill scientific knowledge gaps and to develop a strong knowledge base that can inform decision making and lead to an ICZM, resulting in enhanced environmental, economic, and social resilience in the Yucatán Peninsula. In addition, this report's findings provide compelling arguments to develop specific interventions to tackle the obstacles to environmentally friendly, inclusive, and resilient growth faced by the Yucatán Peninsula.

A major obstacle to confront the peninsula's development challenges is the lack of a formal priority setting mechanism and an adequate institutional framework to align available resources with the most pressing environmental challenges. Using rigorous priority-setting tools, such as the cost of environmental degradation study presented in this report, is an important step to fill this gap. Once environmental priorities have been set, institutional resources should be aligned to address them, and if needed, policies or regulations should be adopted or reformed to efficiently and effectively tackle the issues that are causing the most severe damages. Monitoring and evaluation systems should also be strengthened to assess the extent to which the objectives of environmental priorities are being met. Accumulation of data, results, and experiences in policy design and implementation should be integrated into the Monitoring and Evaluation (M&E) systems to support continuous social learning that underpins further policy improvements.

SMPs are a proven approach to achieve long-term sustainability of coastal risk management for a specific stretch of coast. Developing an SMP includes five main tasks: (a) defining sediment cells as the basic unit for coastal zone management, (b) collating a coastal database designed to support the science within the SMP, (c) developing conceptual (or behavioral) models for each sediment cell, (d) evaluating societal demands on the coast, and (e) reconciling scientific and societal demands within the SMP framework.

To conduct these tasks, the next steps should focus on the collection, storage, and retrieval of coastal data that can be used to develop the conceptual models of the coast. Data should be acquired from both primary and secondary sources. The advantage of using secondary data is that it can reduce both costs and time; however, in many cases secondary data sources are either lacking or inadequate.

The existing database for the Yucatán Peninsula is not considered adequate to support shoreline management. What limited data is available is focused on local issues at scales significantly smaller than those of the sediment cells outlined in the geomorphology sections of this report. This means that management tends to rely on reducing local impacts, rather than seeking general causes of coastal problems. The lack of any data on waves, tides, currents, bathymetry, shoreline topography, and the minimal data on sea level rise must be seen as a major impediment to effective shoreline management. Specific actions are needed to lay the foundations for an information system that can integrate existing and new data to help fill these data gaps.

Given the significant impacts caused by environmental degradation in the Yucatán Peninsula, the environmental information system could also integrate data that will underpin the development of effective and efficient interventions to tackle environmental health risks. Indoor and outdoor air pollution causes the most-significant health impacts. Therefore, the monitoring system should prioritize monitoring of emissions, concentrations and exposure levels to fine particulate matter in outdoor and indoor environments. Initial efforts could focus on monitoring PM2.5, and gradually expand capacity to also monitor PM1.0. The monitoring system should also include a source and composition inventory of the source structure of both primary and secondary PM to guide future air quality management planning and interventions. The monitoring system could also include black carbon emissions, a pollutant linked to PM, with known effects on the climate and on human health.

Improving the knowledge base on lead exposure is also critical because this environmental health risk causes the most significant economic losses in the Yucatán Peninsula. Although blood lead levels have been decreasing over time, efforts should be made to identify and control lead exposure in *hotspots*. In addition, in light of recent evidence of the severity of impacts of lead in children, measurement studies should be undertaken to confirm blood lead levels among children, map geographic pockets of high blood lead levels, and identify and control sources of lead exposure.

In addition to building this information system, steps to address the peninsula's sustainability challenges would include the preparation of pre-feasibility, feasibility, and design studies for specific interventions on coastal management, pollution control, environmental health, and management of natural ecosystems through strengthened management of natural protected areas and Reduced Emissions from Deforestation and Degradation (REDD+). These studies would help to identify the most efficient and effective alternatives to tackle the regional environmental priorities presented in this report.

Two different types of economic losses are associated with the extreme weather events that affect the Yucatán Peninsula. The first includes the relatively modest losses caused by low intensity, but frequently occurring, natural hazards. The second involves the high losses caused by catastrophic events that occur more rarely. Studies should be prepared to assess the adaptation interventions that could be implemented to reduce vulnerability to both kinds of economic losses, recognizing that the benefits and costs of interventions to address the impacts of low intensity events can be quantified with more certainty than those focusing on catastrophic events.

An appropriate way forward is to proceed with a series of pilot projects and interventions, complemented by technical assistance, institutional strengthening, and a scientifically founded M&E program consisting also of appropriate targeted R&D efforts. Table ES.4 summarizes this report's recommendations to help overcome the main obstacles to environmentally healthy, inclusive, and resilient growth faced by the Yucatán Peninsula.

TABLE ES.4 Summary of recommendations

CATEGORY	ACTION	TIME FRAME
Pilot projects and interventions	• Develop pilot projects to control beach erosion in priority sites, using existing information	Short term
	• Replicate pilot projects throughout the peninsula's coastal areas	Medium term
	• Develop shoreline management plans	Medium term
Technical assistance	• Develop pre-feasibility, feasibility, and engineering design and detail studies for coastal erosion, pollution control, and environmental health risk interventions	Short term
Institutional strengthening	• Establish the leadership and institutional arrangements and capacities to set priorities in environmental policy design and implementation	Short term
	• Align environmental expenditure with priorities	Medium term
	• Enhance capacity of environmental agencies on technical, financial, and managerial issues	Medium term
	• Set horizontal and vertical coordination incentives and quantifiable goals	Medium term
	• Strengthen institutional learning and build the necessary feedback loops to mainstream improvements and change	Medium term
Monitoring, evaluation, research, and development	• Generate, collect, and analyze information on waves, tides, currents, bathymetry, shoreline topography, and sea level rise	Short term
	• Establish monitoring networks to monitor atmospheric air pollution in large urban areas, focusing on PM2.5	Short term
	• Establish monitoring networks to monitor indoor air pollution in rural households, focusing on PM2.5	Short term
	• Conduct studies to confirm blood lead levels among children, map geographic pockets of high blood lead levels, and identify and control sources of lead exposure	Short term
	• Expand the information system to include additional data, including water quality, soil quality, and waste management	Medium term

REFERENCES

Diez, J. 2009. "Cancún-Nizuc Coastal Barrier." *Journal of Coastal Research* 25 (1): 57–68.

Gobierno de Yucatán. 2012. *Análisis de la vulnerabilidad actual y futura ante los efectos del cambio climático.* Programa Especial de Acción ante el Cambio Climático del Estado de Yucatán.

González-Leija, M., I. Mariño-Tapia, R. Silva, C. Enriquez, E. Mendoza, E. Escalante-Mancera, F. Ruiz-Renteria, and E. Uc-Sánchez. 2013. "Morphodynamic Evolution and Sediment Transport Processes of Cancún Beach." *Journal of Coastal Research* 29 (5): 1146–57.

Gutierrez-Estrada, M., A. Castro-Del Rio, and A. Galaviz-Solis. 1988. "Mexico". In *Artificial Structures and Shorelines,* edited by H. J. Walker, 669–78. Dordrecht, Netherlands: Kluwer Academic Publishers.

Meyer-Arendt, K. 1991. "Tourism Development on the North Yucatán Coast." *GeoJournal* 23 (4): 327–36.

NOAA (National Ocean and Atmospheric Administration). 2016a. "Historical Hurricane Tracks (Dataset)." http://coast.noaa.gov/hurricanes.

Nordhaus W. D. 2010. "RICE-2010 and DICE-2010 Models (as of August 25, 2010)." http://www.econ.yale.edu/~nordhaus/homepage/RICEmodels.htm.

Abbreviations

Mex$	Mexico Peso 1 Mex$ = US$ 0.054 (September 2017)
ALRI	acute lower respiratory infections
BAU	business as usual
BBL	Broken Bow Lake
BLL	blood lead levels
CAC	command and control
CCA	climate change adaptation
CETM	Compendio Estadístico del Turismo en México (Statistical Compendium of Tourism in Mexico)
CIMARES	Intersecretarial Commission for the Sustainable Management of Seas and Coasts
COI	cost-of-illness
COPD	chronic obstructive pulmonary disease
CZMP	Coastal Zone Management Program
DALY	disability-adjusted life years
EIA	environmental impact assessment
EU	European Union
GDP	gross domestic product
GHG	greenhouse gas
GPA	Global Programme of Action
GRI	gross regional income
ICM	integrated coastal management
ICZM	integrated coastal zone management
INE	Instituto Nacional de Ecología
INECC	National Institute of Ecology and Climate Change
INEGI	Instituto Nacional de Estadística y Geografía
IUCN	International Union for Conservation of Nature
LME	large marine ecosystem
M&E	Monitoring and Evaluation
MBI	market-based instrument
MPA	marine protected area
NOAA	National Oceanic and Atmospheric Administration (the United States)
PB	Lead

PDU	urban development plan
PM	particulate matter
POEGT	Programa de Ordenamiento Ecológico General del Territorio (Territory Ecological Management Programs)
RCP	representative concentration pathway (emission scenario)
SAM	social accounting matrix
SAMEA	social, environmental, and economic accounting matrix
SBP	systolic blood pressure
SD	standard deviation
SEDUMA	Secretariat of Urban Development and Environment (Yucatán)
SEEA03	System of Environmental and Economic Accounting (UN 2003)
SEMA	Secretariat of Ecology and Environment (Quintana Roo)
SEMARNAT	Secretariat of Environment and Natural Resources (Mexico)
SMAAS	Secretariat of Environment and Sustainable Use (Campeche)
SMP	shoreline management plan
UNEP	United Nations Environmental Programme
UNFCCC	United Nations Framework Convention on Climate Change
UNISDR	United Nations Office for Disaster Risk Reduction
UN-REDD	United Nations Programme on Reducing Emissions from Deforestation and Forest Degradation
UN-REDD+	United Nations Programme on Reducing Emissions from Deforestation and Forest Degradation in Developing Countries
VSL	value of a statistical life
WSH	water supply, sanitation, and hygiene
WTP	willingness-to-pay

1 Introduction

ERNESTO SÁNCHEZ-TRIANA, JACK RUITENBEEK, AND SANTIAGO ENRIQUEZ

OVERVIEW

The Yucatán Peninsula comprises the three states of Campeche, Yucatán, and Quintana Roo. Its coast has an extent of 1,941 linear kilometers and has a population of more than 4 million inhabitants. Among these three states, Quintana Roo has the longest coastline, stretching over 1,176 km, followed by Campeche, with a coastline of 425 km. The state of Yucatán, located in the central part of the coast, has the smallest coastal territory, with 340 km (map 1.1) (INEGI 2015).

In Quintana Roo, 10 of the state's 11 municipalities are on the coast; in Campeche, seven of the 11 municipalities are coastal. This is significantly different from the case of Yucatán, where only 13 of its 106 municipalities are located on the coast. In addition, whereas Quintana Roo's and Campeche's coastal areas host each state's main urban centers, most of Yucatán coastal municipalities have populations of less than 10,000. Thus, although Yucatán is the state with the largest total population, coastal populations are much larger in Campeche and Quintana Roo (INEGI 2010a).

In addition to these geographic and demographic variations, there are also important differences in the economic structure of the coastal areas of these three states. In the case of Campeche, mining contributed with more than 83 percent of the state's gross domestic product (GDP) in 2009 (INEGI 2011). Nearly 30 percent of Mexico's fossil fuel reserves are located on the Campeche sound and in the deep sea of the Gulf of Mexico; in the last 30 years, development of these resources has accelerated considerably (Yáñez-Arancibia and Day 2004). Mexico's oil industry contributes an average 30 percent of public net income (BANXICO 2017)[1] and makes Campeche—with its tremendous offshore oil reserves—the fourth-highest contributor to the nation's GDP, contributing 5 percent of Mexico's total GDP. As noted by Villalobos and Rivera (2008), after the discovery and exploitation of oil deposits off the coast of Campeche, PEMEX, the state-owned oil company, established its regional administrative center in Ciudad del Carmen, Campeche. Attracted by the relatively favorable employment opportunities, population grew rapidly and the urban area expanded quickly, particularly between 1970 and 1990. Fishing and aquaculture are also

Map of the Yucatán Peninsula

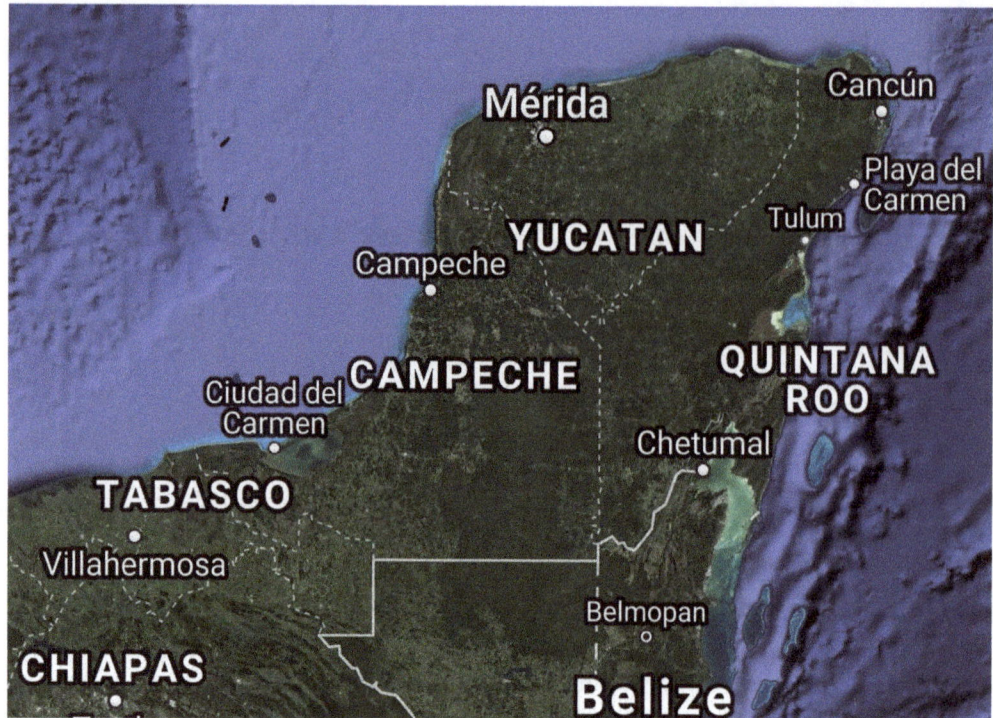

Source: Google maps.

important economic activities, although clearly at a much smaller scale than oil production. Fishing and aquaculture have relative low importance in Mexico, where the sector only accounts for 0.8 percent of the county's GDP. Approximately 14 percent of this takes place in the Gulf of Mexico and the Caribbean. This seems very little, but only four states concentrate 70 percent of the total volume, making Campeche a relative fishing and aquaculture hotspot. Increasing economic activity, coastal and inland, comes with higher demand for ports and marine and land transport.

In the case of Quintana Roo, tertiary activities generated nearly 86 percent of GDP in 2014 (INEGI 2016a). Quintana Roo is the second top tourist destination in Mexico, as evidenced by the nearly 17 million visitors it received in 2017 (more than 17 percent of total tourists for that year). Even though the state received only about 2.8 percent of domestic tourists, the state was the destination of 34.4 percent of the international visitors that traveled to Mexico in 2016 (CETM 2017). Moreover, Quintana Roo captured 33.6 percent of total foreign exchange into the country from tourism in 2016 (SEDETUR 2017). The share of tourism in the Quintana Roo economy is the highest for any state in Mexico. For example, 21.4 percent of the state's GDP is generated by temporary lodging and meal preparation, compared with 2.24 percent at the national level. The predominance of the tourism sector is also clear in other economic variables, including the percentage of jobs, economic units and compensation generated by tourism (INEGI 2016a).

In the state of Yucatán, tertiary activities are also the backbone of the economy, contributing nearly 64 percent of GDP in 2014 (INEGI 2016b). However, in 2016, 78 percent of tourists were domestic and the number of total visitors was significantly smaller, representing about 12 percent of those that visited Quintana Roo during the same year (CETM 2017). Yucatán's archaeological sites are the most visited attraction. In 2017, the state's four main archeological sites (Chichén Itzá, Ek Balám, Uxmal, and Dzibilchaltún) received a total of 3.3 million visitors, which represents an increment of 24 percent in comparison with 2016 (CETM 2017).

ENVIRONMENTAL ISSUES AND PRIORITIES

For the three states of the Yucatán Peninsula, coastal areas underpin the main economic activities. However, the state of environmental management in the peninsula has not kept up with this level of economic activity, both in terms of knowledge production and of regulation. As a result, coastal and marine ecosystems have suffered. Water quality is a major issue in the Yucatán, leading to "problems of human health, eutrophication, harmful algal blooms, fish kills, seagrass loss, coral reef destruction, and even marine mammal and seabird mortality" (Herrera-Silveira et al. 2004).

In addition, climate change could have significant impacts on the Yucatán Peninsula, including an increase in the frequency and intensity of extreme weather events and alteration of marine ecosystems (for example, coral bleaching) (Pech 2010). The Yucatán Peninsula is anticipated to experience the largest increases in temperature in Mexico, and climate change could potentially increase the poverty rate from 15.13 percent to 18.81 percent by 2030 (World Bank 2013). Furthermore, due to its vulnerability to hurricanes, floods and sea level rise, the Yucatán Peninsula is expected to become much more vulnerable to climate events (Borja-Vega and de la Fuente 2013).

Although there are different physical and economic features, the Yucatán Peninsula states are in many ways interdependent. All states benefit from natural and cultural heritage assets that form the backbone to domestic and international tourism. Cooperation has been evident in development of transportation infrastructure. Environmental policies mandated at the Federal level require consistency and harmonization in implementation at the state level. With a population of only 4 million, its future growth prospects will depend on continued cooperation and harmonization of policies that do not undermine the growth potential. Hydrocarbon development in Campeche, for example, must be done with appropriate environmental standards in place such that environmental risks to the Yucatán Peninsula as a whole are not increased. Competition for tourists must not be driven to the point where local carrying capacities are exceeded.

The interdependence of the state economies is acknowledged by all parties, and has been evident in the interest expressed to tackle large problems such as climate change that all states face in common. What has been evident in the lead-up to this cooperation, however, is that there remain substantial gaps in scientific knowledge. In spite of these gaps, many of the priorities in environmental management have already been identified on a preliminary basis. What is not yet clear, however, is the extent of the interconnections among these priorities, or their connection to other policy priorities (such as poverty alleviation, economic diversification, or increased trade). Addressing these interconnections and identifying the appropriate policy approaches, is a long-term challenge that will depend on addressing the scientific gaps, testing different approaches in an adaptive fashion, and sharing experiences over the coming decade to identify and to confront the highest priority issues. In this context, this report summarizes the results of interdisciplinary analytical work that aims to take a first step in filling knowledge gaps by using rigorous methodologies to (a) identify and rank environmental problems; (b) assess policy alternatives to address key sustainable development challenges; and (c) establish a social learning mechanism to identify the shortcomings of proposed interventions and continuously improve them, as well as consider the involvement of different stakeholder groups.

SCOPE AND METHODOLOGY

In response to this challenge, the state governments from the Yucatán Peninsula requested World Bank support to strengthen the knowledge to support coastal management, as well as to take advantage of the region's natural capital to support an economic development that is socially inclusive, clean, efficient, and resilient. In response to this request, the World Bank conducted analytical work and engaged a wide stakeholder base to identify priority issues, assess alternative policies, and lay the foundation to continuously bolster knowledge generation and management in these areas.

The analytical work summarized in this report was conducted by an interdisciplinary team. Economic analysis was used to quantify and prioritize the costs of environmental degradation and natural disasters, which have among the highest impacts on the Yucatán Peninsula. A different type of economic analysis was used to develop a Social Accounting Matrix (SAM) representing the flows of all economic transactions that take place within the Quintana Roo economy. The SAM helped to provide quantitative estimates on the environmental sustainability, economic contributions, and social implications of alternative tourism development scenarios in Quintana Roo. Geomorphological studies helped to assess challenges and opportunities for coastal management in the Yucatán Peninsula, with a view towards addressing current erosion problems and anticipated climate change impacts, such as sea level rise. Policy and institutional analysis underpinned the recommendations presented at the end of this report.

A number of institutions participated in discussions and workshops with the team that conducted the analytical work. These included federal organizations, particularly Mexico's Secretariat of Environment and Natural Resources (SEMARNAT) and the National Institute of Ecology and Climate Change (INECC). At the state level, representatives from Campeche's Secretariat of Environment and Sustainable Use (SMAAS), Quintana Roo's Secretariat of Ecology and Environment (SEMA), and Yucatán's Secretariat of Urban Development and Environment (SEDUMA) provided though leadership and guidance. Academic researchers and representatives from Civil Society Organizations from the Yucatán Peninsula also provided valuable insights and shared ongoing efforts.

The report is organized as follows. Chapter 2 describes the institutional framework for coastal management in the Yucatán Peninsula; within this context, it also provides a general overview of integrated coastal zone management (ICZM) and how Mexico is currently trying to implement it. Chapter 3 discusses the relevance of coastal geomorphology to coastal management, both to address current erosion problems and anticipated climate change impacts, such as sea level rise. It concludes with a discussion of the role of shoreline management plans in coastal management. The report next presents two different economic analyses in areas of high priority and interest identified during stakeholder discussions. Chapter 4 discusses the results of the economic costs of environmental degradation in the Yucatán Peninsula, focusing particularly on the historic impacts of natural disasters and their potential effects in the context of future climate change. Chapter 5 summarizes the results of an analysis conducted to identify and rank the environmental problems that cause the most severe social and economic impacts in the Yucatán Peninsula. Chapter 6 analyzes the structure of Quintana Roo's economy, the impacts of tourism development for different economic sectors, and opportunities to shift towards a tourism model that fosters social inclusion, and conservation and restoration of natural capital. Chapter 7 treats the potential role of environmental impact assessment (EIA) as a means to achieve integrated shoreline management and environmentally sustainable development; EIA is already considerably developed, but would need some reforms to be a useful tool in the ICZM context. Most significantly, EIA needs to be strengthened with regard to demands on project developers, and EIA needs to accommodate adaptive measures in its regulatory structure. Chapter 8 presents conclusions.

NOTE

1. Based on monthly data from January 2000 through September 2017.

REFERENCES

BANXICO (Banco de México). 2017. *Sistema de Información Económica*. Online query, conducted on November 21, 2017.

Borja-Vega, C., and A. de la Fuente. 2013. *Municipal Vulnerability to Climate Change and Climate-Related Events in Mexico*. Policy Research Working Paper 6417, A World Bank Study, World Bank, Washington, DC. https://openknowledge.worldbank.org/handle/10986/15560. License: CC BY 3.0 IGO.

Carranza-Edwards, A., A. P. Marín-Guzmán, and L. Rosales-Hoz. 2010. "Problemática ambiental en la gestión costera-marina." In *Cambio climático en México: Un enfoque costero y marino*, edited by E. Rivera-Arriaga, I. Azuz-Adeath, L. Alpuche Gual, and G. J. Viallobos-Zapata. Campeche: Universidad Autónoma de Campeche, CETYS-Universidad, Gobierno del Estado de Campeche.

CETM (Compendio Estadístico del Turismo en México). 2017. Ciudad de México, México: Secretaría de Turismo. http://www.datatur.sectur.gob.mx/Documentos%20compartidos/CETM2017.zip

Herrera-Silveira, J. A., F. A. Comin, N. Aranda-Cirerol, L. Troccoli, and L. Capurro. 2004. "Coastal Water Quality Assessment in the Yucatán Peninsula: Management Implications." *Ocean & Coastal Management* 47 (11): 625–39.

INEGI (Instituto Nacional de Estadística y Geografía).

——. 2010b. *Censo Económico 2009*. Aguascalientes, Mexico: INEGI.

——. 2011. *Sistema de Cuentas Nacionales de México: Producto interno bruto por entidad federativa 2005–2009: Año base 2003*. Aguascalientes, Mexico: INEGI.

——. 2015. *Anuario estadístico y geográfico por entidad federativa 2015*. Aguascalientes, Mexico: INEGI.

——. 2016a. Estructura económica de Quintana Roo en síntesis, Mexico: INEGI.

——. 2016b. Estructura económica de Yucatán en síntesis, Mexico: INEGI.

Pech, D. 2010. "Cambio climático global, eventos extremos y biodiversidad costera de la península de Yucatán." In *Cambio Climático en México: un enfoque costero y marino*, edited by E. Rivera-Arriaga, I. Azuz-Adeath, L. Alpuche Gual, and G. J. Viallobos-Zapata. Campeche: Universidad Autónoma de Campeche, CETYS-Universidad, Gobierno del Estado de Campeche.

SEDETUR (Secretaría de Turismo del Estado de Quintana Roo). 2017. *Indicadores Turísticos Enero - Diciembre 2017* (accessed November 7, 2018), http://sedeturqroo.gob.mx /ARCHIVOS/indicadores/Indicadores%20Tur%20-%20Diciembre%202017.pdf.

Villalobos, M., C. Merino-Sánchez, C. Hall, J. Grieshop, M. E. Gutiérrez-Ruiz, and M. A. Handley. 2009. "Lead (II) Detection and Contamination Routes in Environmental Sources, Cookware and Home-Prepared Foods from Zimatlán, Oaxaca, Mexico." *The Science of the Total Environment* 407: 2836–44.

World Bank. 2013. *Las Dimensiones Sociales del Cambio Climático en México*. A World Bank Study. Washington, DC: World Bank. http://www.bancomundial.org/content/dam /Worldbank/document/web%20spa%20mexico.pdf.

Yáñez-Arancibia, A., and J. W. Day. 2004. "The Gulf of Mexico: Towards an Integration of Coastal Management with Large Marine Ecosystem Management." *Ocean & Coastal Management* 47 (11): 537–63.

2 Institutional Considerations for Coastal Management in the Yucatán Peninsula

JACK RUITENBEEK AND JOHN PETHICK

INTRODUCTION

Mexico's environmental management framework is inadequate to address the large-scale impacts of economic activities in the Yucatán Peninsula. In the case of offshore mining operations, Mexico has a number of environmental regulations governing the construction and operation of these projects; however, several areas are either absent or under-enforced. For example, public participation is extremely underutilized: public comments were incorporated into only 19 percent of the cases studied by Hernández et al. (2012). Additionally, there is virtually no scope, within the Mexican governmental framework, for the states to take a role in managing oil industry activities. Overall, Mexico's legal infrastructure only contains half the requirements that would be needed to create a regulatory environment conducive to sustainable operation of the oil industry. For coastal tourism in Quintana Roo and for the fishing industry along the Yucatán coast, this number is even lower: 36 percent and 25 percent respectively (Hernández et al. 2012; Vidal and Capurro-Filigrasso 2008).

There are also a number of gaps regarding knowledge production. For instance, while development of offshore oil reserves proceeds apace, there is little knowledge as to the impact of these activities upon the marine environment. There have been studies, largely inconclusive, of the effect of the presence of fossil fuel sediment within the water. However, there have been no long-term studies of the effect of pollution or other impacts associated with other phases of the activity: construction, noise, transport, air quality, excavation, and so forth (Hernández et al. 2012). Most of the research in the fisheries sector has been focused on how to conserve individual species, rather than on how to consider broader ecosystem linkages (Garcia 2003; Ortiz-Lozano et al. 2007).

In recent years, academics and planners have recognized that regulations alone are not enough to provide for the sustainable future of the coastal and marine ecosystems of the Yucatán Peninsula. Even if each oilrig or fishing boat were operated according to regulation, the overall development of the region would still entail potential ecosystem impacts. The resulting strategy coordinates usage of land, water, and national resources with a view to maintaining biodiversity and preserving the overall health and resilience of the ecosystem (Maltby 2003). On an international level, this approach is often reflected in the integrated management of coastal and marine ecosystems.

ROLE OF INTEGRATED COASTAL ZONE MANAGEMENT

History of Integrated Coastal Zone Management (ICZM)

Coasts have always been valuable zones of habitation both for human beings and for valuable flora and fauna. Approximately 44 percent of humanity lives within 150 km of a coast (UN 2010). As such, coastal systems include the biomes that are most vulnerable to impacts from economic development (Lindeboom 2002). In the past several decades, there has been increasing interest in maintaining the natural biodiversity and the valuable ecosystem services of these regions, even in the face of increasing development (Dietz, Ostrom, and Stern 2003).

Habitation in coastal areas is, however, nothing new and people have been dealing with changes in coastal systems since time immemorial. The United Nations estimates that 44 percent of people in the world live within 150 km of the coast. As depicted in figure 2.1, 50,000 years of such habitation has implicitly generated a long history of integrated coastal management through which human populations have adapted to and modified coastal systems. The timeline demonstrates simply that people have been dealing with changes in the coastal regions for a long time. Going back 50,000 years, human populations have suffered through floods, changes in sea level, droughts, wetting periods and drying periods. People have adapted to this through hard engineering, such as dikes and embankments, changes in diet, diversification and many types of adaptation.

FIGURE 2.1
50,000 years of ICZM

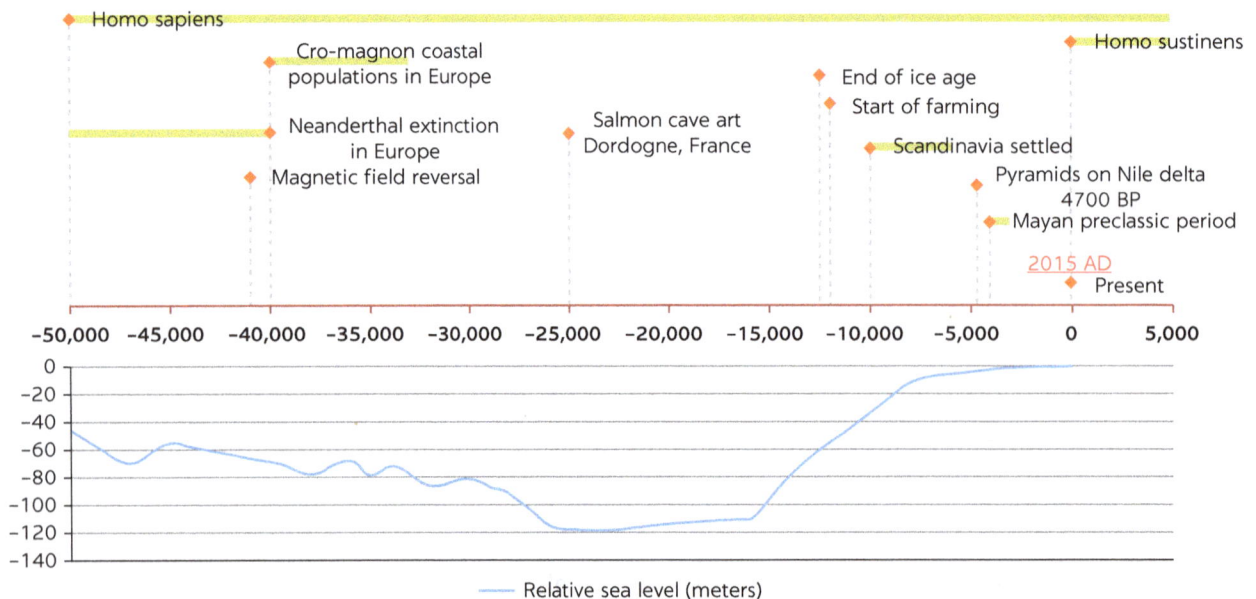

Note: Sea level is eustatic based on IPCC (2007) and Lambeck and Chappell (2001). ICZM = integrated coastal zone management.

Notably, people have moved with the seashore. This period includes geological time: over the past 50,000 years, there have been glaciation events, a flip in the earth's magnetic field, loss of Neanderthals, and evolution of *Homo sapiens* (the "wise man") in a way that brings us to the present. Moving forward, some argue that humanity will need to evolve to become "sustainable human being"—*Homo sustinens*—to continue to adapt in a world of increasing population and vulnerable resources.

Modern process-oriented ICZM is frequently considered to have started in San Francisco in 1965, followed shortly by the U.S. Coastal Zone Management Act. However, the timeline in figure 2.2 highlights that major works using process-oriented methods were also conceived prior to 1965. For example, approaches in the Netherlands show a heavy engineering response of Dutch ICZM before *Modern ICZM* was ever started. That engineering includes putting in dikes that turned it into polders, which is land useful for settlement and agriculture. The development of polders can be seen throughout Europe however: they are found in the UK and other countries of mainland Europe. Bangladesh has also adopted the polder practice over the past decades. All of the engineering in the Netherlands, however, was to protect people and assets: devastating floods in 1916 and 1953 resulted in what are now arguably the strongest coastal defenses in the world.

As shown in figure 2.3, international norms were elaborated through the Noordwijk Guidelines in 1993. European countries started policies of *managed realignment* in the 1990s: This involved abandoning to the sea areas that were previously inhabited, in order to achieve a more naturally resilient coastal zone.

FIGURE 2.2

Context of ICZM events

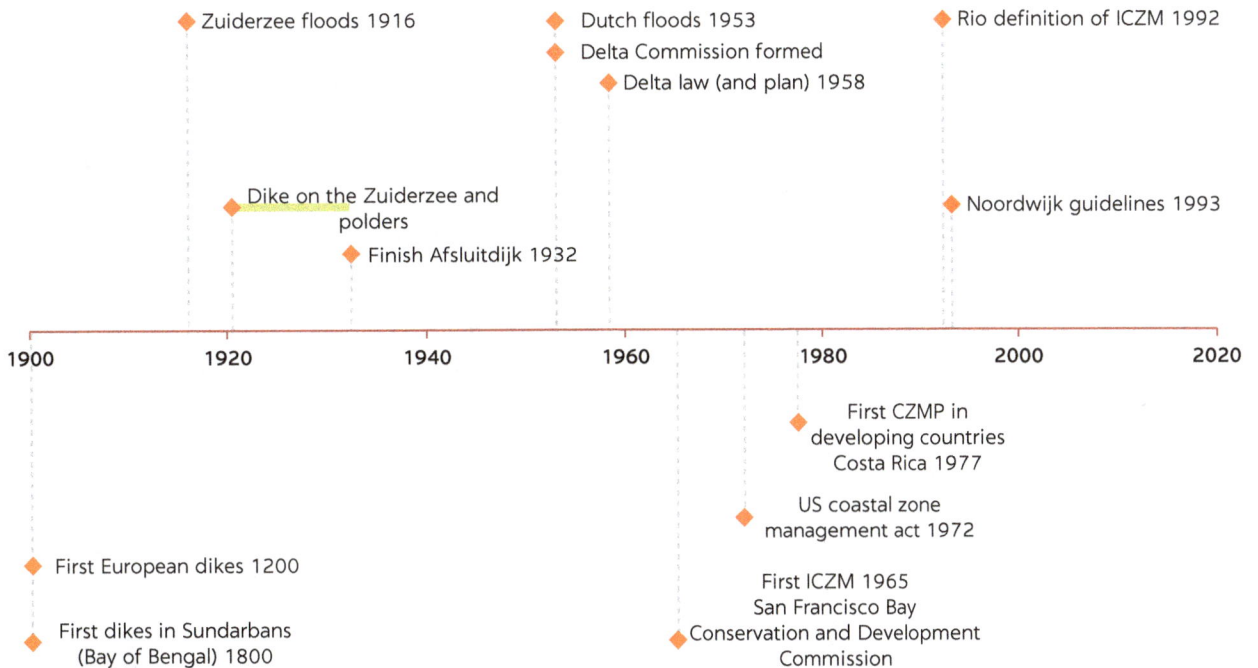

Note: CZMP = Coastal Zone Management Program; ICZM = integrated coastal zone management.

FIGURE 2.3

Key modern ICZM events: 1965–2015

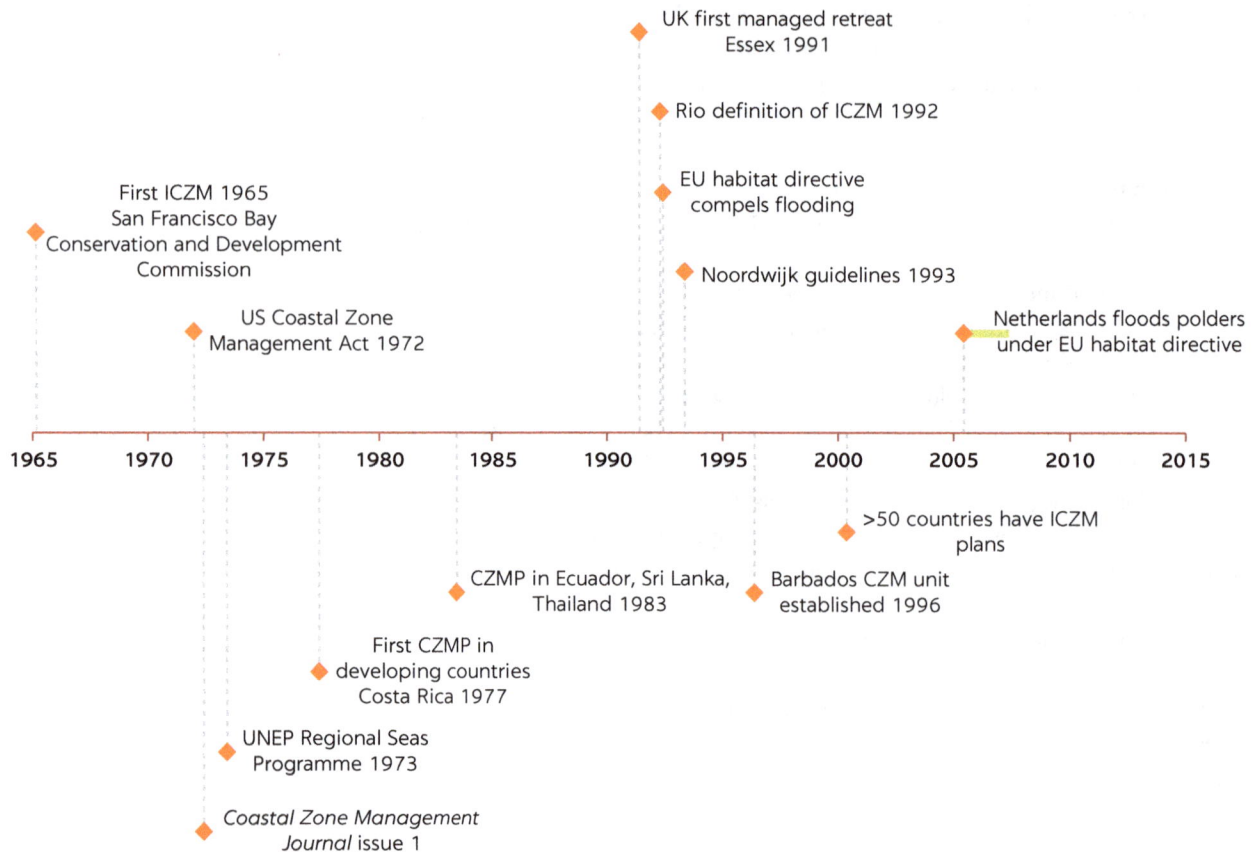

Note: CZMP = Coastal Zone Management Program; ICZM = integrated coastal zone management; UNEP = United Nations Environment Programme.

Preliminary definitions and insights

ICZM defined

The Global Programme of Action (GPA), developed by the United Nations Environmental Programme (UNEP), is an example of a traditional ICZM approach. It involves (a) an initial assessment of conditions, (b) an assessment of risks and constraints involved in addressing underlying problems, (c) formulation of cost-effective interventions, (d) implementation of interventions, and (e) monitoring and evaluation of effectiveness (UNEP/GPA 2006). Such process orientation is a key aspect of modern ICZM that encourages learning cycles. More-rigorous attempts at definition have resulted in characterizations such as the following, which the European Union (European Environment Agency CEC Communication 2000/547 ICZM)[1] uses:

> Integrated coastal zone management (ICZM) is a dynamic, multidisciplinary and iterative process to promote sustainable management of coastal zones. It covers the full cycle of information collection, planning (in its broadest sense), decision making, management and monitoring of implementation. ICZM uses the informed participation and cooperation of all stakeholders to assess the societal goals in a given coastal area, and to take actions towards meeting these objectives. ICZM seeks, over the long-term, to balance environmental, economic, social, cultural and recreational objectives, all within the limits set by natural dynamics. "Integrated" in ICZM refers to the integration of objectives and also to the integration of the many instruments

needed to meet these objectives. It means integration of all relevant policy areas, sectors, and levels of administration. It means integration of the terrestrial and marine components of the target territory, in both time and space.

Many Latin American governments have instituted sectoral approaches to environmental development: individual laws and procedures for measuring and mitigating environmental impacts in individual sectors (tourism, mining, agricultural, and so forth). However, these laws lead to an *ad hoc* approach and fail to capture the cumulative impacts of all associated activities. Many have argued for a more integrated approach, which comprehensively monitors and set priorities for a given ecosystem (Saturnino et al. 2008). In defining Integrated Coastal Management, Yáñez-Arancibia and Day (2004) are more specific in some of the goals but provide a definition that is similar to that of the EU:

> ICM is a dynamic process by which decisions are taken for the use, development and protection of coastal areas and resources, to achieve goals established in cooperation with user groups and authorities. ICM recognizes the distinctive character of the coastal zone, is multiple-purpose-oriented, analyzes implications of development, conflicting uses, and interrelationships between physical processes and human activities, and promotes linkages and harmonization among sectoral, coastal and ocean activities. There are at least seven different kinds of integration: (a) intergovernmental, (b) land-water interface, (c) intersectoral, (d) interdisciplinary, (e) interinstitutional, (f) intertemporal, and (g) managerial.

Other regions have been more precise in their definitions. The state of Victoria in Australia regards ICZM as one of the three parts that contribute to an overarching idea of *ecologically sustainable development*. Other blocks include Ecosystem Based Management and Adaptive Management. Their specific understanding of ICZM follows (see Victorian Coastal Council 2014):

> A framework that attempts to integrate planning and management in a region, such as the State of Victoria, across the land and sea interface and the private and public land interface, to treat the coastal zone (which includes the catchment) as one biophysical entity.

All of the above definitions have a number of elements in common. Specifically, they involve

- Elements of *stocktaking and diagnostic exercises*, often involving new and ongoing research
- Explicit or implicit *objective setting*
- *Participation* of multiple stakeholders
- *Priority setting*—often with economic valuation –, regarded as necessary at the beginning and throughout the process
- *Sectoral integration*, as opposed to traditional sector-oriented processes and
- *Learning and feedback* that contribute to ongoing adaptation.

In addition, the more recent ICZM approaches have also focused on

- Addressing the *reduction of vulnerability* under uncertainty: precisely because of scientific gaps that cannot necessarily be filled within the required policy-making time horizons and

- Incorporation of ideas of the *global commons* in the integration of global fishery issues, greenhouse gas (GHG) emission reduction, and other issues that extend beyond a simple coastal stretch.

The Noordwijk ICZM Guidelines (World Bank 1996) provide a codified manual for following an ICZM process. They are based on the Rio Agenda 21 (chapter 17) outcomes of 1992 and were first developed by interested parties in a meeting in Noordwijk Netherlands in 1993 (UNSD 1992). Subsequent refinements by the World Bank over the period 1993–96 provide a useful starting point for ICZM program implementation. The guidelines include the following specific objectives:

1) Strengthen Sectoral Management. This is conducted through a variety of means including (a) training and awareness building for decision makers, (b) reforms and activities in key coastal sectors, (c) efforts to achieve sectoral coordination and cooperation, and (d) identification of actionable policies (such as removal of distortionary economic policies that contribute to pollution)
2) Protect Coastal Ecosystems. This objective is actionable and involves (a) a "ridge to reef" approach, capable of addressing issues related to fisheries, coral reefs, beaches, dunes, seagrass beds, mudflats, riparian systems, coastal lagoons, and upper watersheds; and (b) prevention of damage to such systems and, if needed, their restoration
3) Promotion of Rational Development. This involves programs aimed at (a) risk reduction, (b) mitigation for human and ecosystem health, and (c) design and implementation of appropriate regulatory and incentive mechanisms. A new emergent objective includes (d) the development of *green cities*.

The guidelines also feature the following general principles:

- Adhere to Precautionary Principle: the principle that the introduction of a new product or process whose ultimate effects are disputed or unknown should be resisted
- Adhere to Polluter Pay Principle: the principle that whoever is responsible for any form of pollution or environmental damage should be responsible for covering the full costs of such damage, or for avoiding the costs of such damage
- Conduct Proper Resource Accounting: attach economic value to ecosystem goods and services, and potentially to natural assets
- Acknowledge Transboundary Responsibility: cooperate where possible in areas of mutual interest and
- Respect Intergenerational Equity: do not limit options of future generations.

Coastal zones in the broader landscape

ICZM is compatible with numerous other methods of and approaches to spatial planning in a broader landscape. Ecosystem-based management and watershed management approaches have been espoused as a way of respecting natural landscapes in planning, in contrast to more-traditional boundaries that typically relied on convenient political and sectoral boundaries. Indeed, the greatest challenges for all such approaches is that the planning processes (including budgeting, financing, and regulation) remain constrained by political boundaries associated with nations, states, counties, parishes or similar political, sectoral, or socially determined borders. By explicitly recognizing these institutional constraints, however, ICZM seeks to balance the socioeconomic realities with the natural biophysical realities.

In that respect, ICZM is very compatible with a more recently elaborated "landscape approach". As described by the World Bank (World Bank 2016a):

[a] "landscape approach" means taking both a geographical and socioeconomic approach to managing the land, water and forest resources that form the foundation—the natural capital—for meeting our goals of food security and inclusive green growth.

The World Bank Group is increasingly employing landscape approaches to implement strategies that integrate management of land, water, and living resources, and that promote sustainable use and conservation in an equitable manner. By taking into account the interactions between these core elements of natural capital and the ecosystem services they produce, rather than considering them in isolation from one another, we are better able to maximize productivity, improve livelihoods, and reduce negative environmental impacts. Put more simply: we can "use natural capital without using it up."

That said, a coordinated multi-sectoral perspective is required: a "landscape approach" that provides the organizing principle for investing in and managing land, water, and forest resources based on rational spatial planning and socioeconomic considerations (World Bank 2016b).

In partnership with the World Bank, Mexico has also embarked on a program to improve forest management within such a landscape approach. As the forests are both inland and coastal, such initiatives can eventually provide an important basis for further developing more comprehensive ICZM approaches.

Such an approach ensures activities in other sectors such as agriculture, transport, mining, or hydropower are undertaken in ways that limit impacts on forest and other natural resources integrity at the same time they maximize development benefits.

Insights

In terms of drawing lessons from ICZM, in many cases it is "too early to tell". ICZM is by its nature an intergenerational undertaking. Many regard some of the early experiences in the United States and Europe to be successful, but there too, more-recent advances in coastal management have seen, for example, the promotion of managed retreat or realignment of shorelines. This process abandons decades, or even centuries, of efforts to use hard defenses as a management mechanism. However, even such backtracking can be interpreted as a success; it shows that decision making adapts as new information is made available.

Notwithstanding the difficulty in drawing conclusions regarding ICZM, some general lessons are evident and can be summarized as follows:

- Most ICZM weaknesses relate to institutional breakdowns, delays or inadequate financing
- The process itself can become a burden and source of conflict: choose a few elements. Most ICZM processes describe very complex systems that interact, but that does not imply that the responses need to be complex, although bureaucracies frequently seem to prefer a complex solution
- Assess institutional factors carefully before deciding on single *vs* multiple institutions. The original Noordwijk Guidelines recommended that a single institution to address coastal issues is the best way forward (World Bank 1996). While some positive examples are available (Barbados), the single institution approach has not generally worked in larger contexts because it

just adds one more layer of bureaucracy to what is often already a complicated institutional setting
- Laws tend not to be adaptive: write them carefully
- Economic valuation helps in priority setting. The approaches to valuation have been found useful by policymakers the world over. Waite, Burke and Gray (2014) recently published a manual and case studies of relevance in the Caribbean context
- Market based incentives work, but so do regulations. Before pursuing either, however, one should remove perverse incentives first. A perverse incentive is an economic signal intended to improve conditions in one sector, but that works against the objectives of sound coastal zone management.

In addition, the following findings may be more controversial, but have also become part of the reality of ICZM in some countries:

- Do not presume that historically slow changes will continue to be slow: systems flip. Coral bleaching is an example where massive bleaching events resulted in coral deaths in tourism hot spots around the world
- Encourage risk taking, experimentation, and innovation. This is part of adaptive management, but is a major barrier in many institutions worldwide. Incentive structures are generally designed to do exactly the opposite
- Acknowledge that people may need to move, or that a historically possible activity is no longer viable. For example, various locations around the world have embarked on programs of managed realignment that permit the sea to reclaim previously inhabited areas. In some regions (the Black Sea and Varadero, Cuba), hotels built on dunes have been destroyed as part of these efforts
- ICZM can still incorporate conservation, development, restoration, conversion, and hard engineering. There is an incorrect view that ICZM is entirely conservation–oriented but, more correctly, it should be regarded as process oriented and capable of addressing both conservation and development needs and making necessary trade-offs along the way. A fundamental aspect of ICZM is that it is based on valid information, which all parties can scrutinize before making decisions. Such decisions still provide scope for hard engineering solutions.

The World Bank has also had recent experience in implementing ICZM initiatives. Assistance to India has encompassed a US$285.67 million initiative with general objectives of building national capacity for implementation of a comprehensive coastal management approach in the country, and of piloting the ICZM approach in the states of Gujarat, Odisha, and West Bengal.[2] The project was initiated in 2010, and the following practical lessons can be drawn from that experience that are relevant to further initiatives in India as well as new initiatives elsewhere in the world:

- Clear subsidiarity must be established: responsibility (for implementation) should reside at the most effective and appropriate level, for reasons of (a) political legitimacy, (b) administrative efficiency, and (c) substantive issues related to the nature of cross-sectoral sustainability problems. Conflicting interests in practical implementation can only be resolved if those stakeholders with an active interest in outcomes are also involved in implementation
- There is no cookbook implementation arrangement that fits all problems. Traditionally, three types of arrangements have been used and each has advantages and disadvantages: (a) expanding the duties of an existing agency,

(b) concentrating authority in a new agency, and (c) creating an inter-ministerial council or interagency coordinating committee with a lead agency

- Whichever implementation arrangement is followed, the arrangement will be most successful under the following conditions: (a) skillsets include integration/program management as opposed to specialized technical skills; (b) capacity must be put in place to respond quickly and to handle a wide array of management tasks (contracting, finance, accounting, monitoring and reporting, public communication, budgeting, and transparent approval processes); and (c) a shared long-term vision is founded based on a scientifically sound common knowledge base

- The majority of ICZM projects underestimate the financial resources needed because of the complex nature of coastal processes that result in implementation delays and the frequent need to expand the scope of activities as work progresses

- Monitoring and evaluation within ICZM projects must be actively pursued from the start, and needs to be a core ongoing activity within any project management unit or similar agency.

ICZM IN MEXICO

Current policy instruments

Few countries have the formal regulatory structures that permit comprehensive management of large spaces and sensitive ecosystems in an integrated manner. In Mexico, command-and-control regulations based on a sectoral approach exist, as do other piecework environmental regulations, but there is no structure to tie together various jurisdictions and ministries and coordinate their actions, let alone coordinate among different sectors for ICZM.

In the past, the Mexican Government has recognized the importance of promoting an integrated policy for marine and coastal areas. However, other perspectives and sectoral priorities have subdued the development and integration of such policy. To illustrate this point, the Mexican government created in June 2008 the Intersecretarial Commission for the Sustainable Management of Seas and Coasts (CIMARES). The Commission adopted in 2012 the National Policy for Mexican Seas and Coasts, with three overarching objectives: (a) improving the living conditions of coastal populations, (b) strengthening local economies and strengthening regional competitiveness, and (c) ensuring the structure and functioning of marine-coastal ecosystems (CIMARES 2012). The objectives of this policy were incorporated into Mexico's National Development Plan for 2013–18. However, available information indicates that CIMARES met only once under the 2012–18 Federal Administration.[3]

Nevertheless, concerning the regulatory framework, something approaching ICZM is undertaken in Mexico largely through three policy instruments: (a) Environmental Impact Assessment, (b) the creation of Marine Protected Zones, and (c) ecological zoning (Creel 2005; Hernández et al. 2012).

Environmental impact assessment

Mexico requires all projects to submit an environmental impact assessment if they fall under the categories mentioned in the EIA regulations. These EIAs are a tool for (a) opening up projects to public scrutiny, (b) analyzing possible negative impacts, and (c) mandating mitigations for those impacts (Ortega-Rubio et al. 2001). In terms of coastal management and generally speaking, EIAs can be either project focused or regionally focused. When they are project-focused, they narrowly target the impacts of a particular site: a new oil rig, for instance. When they are regionally focused, they look at potential impacts of an entire enterprise—a new oil field, for instance—within the context of the other economic activities taking place within the broader ecosystem (Hernández et al. 2012). As for Mexico, regional EIAs are an exception: the majority of EIAs presented are project-based. In a recent case study carried out for priority sites in the Yucatán Peninsula, none of the EIAs available during the last 10 years was regional.

EIAs have been used as a method for assessing cumulative impacts of activities in coastal zones (Kennedy 1994). However, assessing such cumulative impacts is difficult because of the scale and the number of considerations involved. Furthermore, it becomes necessary, when looking at cumulative impacts, to begin taking into account social, economic, and political forces (Matishov Denisov and Kirillova 1998).

Under traditional EIA, the impact of one activity upon another activity is a major consideration. For instance, an EIA might measure the impact of oil production upon the local fisheries. However, a cumulative impact assessment measures the impact of all economic activities in the area (Matishov Denisov and Kirillova 1998).

There are two major approaches to cumulative impact assessment. The first is primarily scientific and analytical. Under this approach, the purpose of the assessment is to make estimations and predictions regarding current and future activities in the region and, under best scientific practices, to develop a general understanding of what the expected impacts of these activities might be and how policy makers could mitigate them. The second approach, in contrast, views the assessment primarily as a tool for revealing priorities within the region. Under this approach, the assessment is used as a priority-setting tool to elicit public comment and participation by stakeholders. Scientific knowledge production is still a component of the assessment, but the knowledge is produced in concert with affected groups. Their concerns influence the production of knowledge and the production of knowledge in turn influences their concerns (Kennedy 1994).

In Mexico, significant capacity and regulatory gaps hinder the implementation of EIA in general, and in particular, hinder its implementation for cumulative impacts. EIA practice in Mexico has a number of limitations. These include inadequate scoping, elaboration of environmental impact studies based on incomplete data, insufficient participation from external experts in the Manifestación de Impacto Ambiental (MIA, or Environmental Impact Study) preparation and evaluation, faulty public participation, absence of clear criteria to evaluate the MIA, and weak enforcement and follow-up to ensure that the project developer complies with all the requirements that SEMARNAT established during the EIA process. Chapter 7 presents a more detailed discussion of Mexico's EIA practices. In brief, Mexico's EIA system in its current form is not well suited for coastal zone management.

Ecological zoning program

Mexico's Ecological Zoning Program is promising. Through a consultative process, stakeholders can agree upon a set of requirements for development in a given ecological area. All subsequent projects are then, through the EIA regulation, required to adhere to these requirements. Territorial Environmental Land Use Programs (*Programas de Ordenamiento Ecológico General del Territorio* or POEGTs) are regional development plans developed through participatory processes in which local, state, and federal government stakeholders, as well as civil society and academics, come together in a process designed to maximize consensus. These instruments have been extensively used in Mexico, including throughout the Yucatán Peninsula, but results have been mixed. A POEGT could be potentially complemented by an urban development plan (PDU), which is developed in a similar manner. However, synergies between these two types of planning instruments are rarely built, largely because they fall under the purview of different agencies. Like POEGTs, PDUs are sometimes hampered by a lack of technical and institutional capacity within local and municipal governments for overseeing the complex tasks involved in assessing environmental needs, setting priorities, and building consensus among stakeholders (Creel 2005; Hardoy et al. 2014). There is also a certain level of unwieldiness to the creation of a POEGT. They are developed through a participatory process that a consultant manages, which means that one stakeholder can cause significant roadblocks. Because of this, the resulting agreements tend not to be as strong as would be desired. In addition, to have legal validity, POEGTs must be approved by a decree from the authority at the competent level—federal, state, or municipal. To date, there have been no rigorous attempts to evaluate the effectiveness and efficiency of the preparation and enforcement of POEGTs, most of which lack an appropriate monitoring and evaluation framework (INE 2012). For the Yucatán Peninsula, there are three regional and 10 municipal POEGTs,[4] but some large areas are not yet covered by a POEGT. Specifically, Campeche's coastal zone lacks a regional POEGT, and in Quintana Roo, only the Sian Ka'an region is covered by a regional POEGT. Within the Yucatán Peninsula, only Yucatán's coast is entirely covered by a regional program. In fact, most of Mexico's coastal zones lack a POEGT. However, these plans are a valuable consensus-making tool and provide one of the best ways of formalizing the agreements that need to be made if various municipalities, states, and ministries are going to work together.

Marine protected areas

Mexico has 177 Natural Protected Areas, out of which nearly 70 span over marine or coastal ecosystems. There has been debate over how to use these marine protected areas (MPAs) as an avenue for ICZM. In general, within Mexico, the designation of a marine protected zone has also often included an influence zone, which has acknowledged environmental and socioeconomic ties to a specific protected area. However, protected area officials often have limited influence on development or management of the influence zone.

In general, there has been interest from policy makers, protected area managers, and other stakeholders to find some way to achieve better integration and co-management. Such coordination would allow those in charge of planning zones to be cognizant of their effect on nearby protected ecosystems and to create policies with those ecosystems in mind. ICZM advocates want to use the scale and the popularity of MPAs—there is far more area under protected status than under anything approaching integrated management—to create larger ICZM initiatives. MPA advocates want to build upon the protected area concept by creating linkages between different MPAs and creating an understanding that the entire Gulf of Mexico is one large ecosystem (Cicin-Sain and Belfiore 2005).

Indeed, ecological processes within the marine environment of the Gulf cannot be separated from those occurring along the coast and within the river systems. Everything is connected, but no overall plan for managing the health of the gulf currently exists. A challenge is to integrate coastal zone management with Large Marine Ecosystems (LME) management, and to develop plans that take into account the health of the entire gulf (Yanez-Arancibia et al. 2013).

CLIMATE CHANGE ADAPTATION AND MITIGATION

The United Nations Framework Convention on Climate Change (UNFCCC) recognizes a host of potential policy responses to the threats and consequences of climate changes. *Mitigation* measures are intended to reduce the pace or degree of climate change: typical policy measures are associated with mechanisms that reduce GHG emissions or offset such emissions through activities that absorb or lock up carbon dioxide or other GHGs. Afforestation, reforestation, composting, CO_2, or methane storage are all examples of activities that represent mitigation efforts. Some of these activities also have joint benefits: for example, the United Nations Collaborative Programme on Reducing Emissions from Deforestation and Forest Degradation in Developing Countries (UN-REDD+) is also intended to meet certain social goals and to improve biodiversity. Mitigation programs in coastal communities worldwide have taken advantage of economic incentives to plant mangroves, institute composting, and promote conservation of seagrass beds.

By contrast, *adaptation* measures include activities that may be necessary to cope with the impacts of current or future climate change. Climate change adaptation (CCA) can be targeted to fire risks, droughts, flooding, pests, extreme weather events, increased acidity or temperatures in marine systems, changes in the food-supply chain, or preparedness for a host of uncertain impacts. In coastal regions, sea level rise may also be a concern. An important context for CCA is that these impacts have been occurring since time immemorial: floods, droughts, collapses of food stocks, and other hazards are all a part of human history. To a significant degree, formal and informal mechanisms have been in place for some time to adapt to our changing environment. What is perhaps unprecedented is that the time frames for adaptation may be more immediate than heretofore experienced. Furthermore, the scale of environmental change may not be one to which many of these mechanisms are accustomed. For example, migration away from a dangerous coast has always been the only option for some cultures. However, modern cities, industries, and populations are more likely to harden coastal defenses than to move away from the coast. While migration remains an available coping strategy, most CCA efforts over the next century will be dedicated to a host of other activities integrated into public and private investment decisions, and into how human populations interact with the broader systems making up the coastal environment.

Mexico has been proactive in addressing climate change. The country's mitigation strategy is one of the strongest and most developed among middle- and low-income countries. In terms of adaptation, the country is still in the planning stages: addressing capacity and designing interventions. Under the climate change law, Mexico intends to alter patterns of development with a view to limiting vulnerability. The law would also conserve ecosystems to retain natural barriers to cyclones and other climate events. However, these intentions have not yet been acted upon (Hardoy et al. 2014). In Quintana Roo, authorities are taking proactive steps, through a cross-cutting Office of Climate Change, to enact policies for altering land use in coastal areas and for mitigating disaster risk. In many cases, the practices undertaken as part of climate change initiatives—particularly the changes in land use—are similar to those that would be undertaken through ICZM. However, efforts are hampered by the difficulty of managing participatory processes, by the distribution of responsibilities among many different agencies, and by the lack of specific funding allocated to climate change adaptation (Hardoy et al. 2014). A first step has been taken to overcome those hurdles by the creation of the Regional Climate Change Commission for the Yucatán Peninsula, a joint committee that the three states created to coordinate efforts on climate change mitigation and adaptation. The commission still faces several challenges, including lack of a solid jurisdictional mandate and institutionalization, absence of funding for the institution itself, and limited availability of funds for specific interventions.

It is acknowledged that, for Yucatán Peninsula states, adaptation issues are more pressing than mitigation issues. The Yucatán Peninsula's population of more than 4 million will have limited influence over national GHG emissions, although they may benefit from economic incentives associated with UNFCCC and related programs. The greater focus on adaptation is a natural consequence of the perceived increase in climate-related threats: hurricanes, beach erosion, mangrove loss, coral bleaching, fishery collapses, and fires can all be conveniently classified to some degree as *climate change impacts*. However, with the exception of hurricane intensity, frequency, and timing of incidence, all these impacts may also be related to other influences over which local authorities have some control. Beach erosion may be related to settlement patterns and improper construction on dunes. Loss of mangroves may be related to settlement patterns and incentives that promote conversion. Coral bleaching may be aggravated by eutrophication and land-based pollution. Fishery collapses may be associated with inappropriate use of gear or unsustainable levels of effort rather than changes in environmental conditions. Most fires in the world are the result of human actions. In short, while this implies that many climate impacts may have nothing to do with climate, it does show that there is significant scope for intervention to adapt because some of these impacts may be caused by local actions. Concretely, this implies that CCA and its associated activities must be woven into multiple aspects of ongoing decisions across a broad range of areas. In the coastal zone, almost any approach to CCA can build synergies with ICZM.

CCA and ICZM efforts and institutional structures are highly complementary. A successful climate change strategy, particularly in a coastal area, strongly resembles ICZM, in that a successful CC strategy (a) requires coordination among all sectors and departments in an area, (b) addresses the need to maximize resilience by guiding development in sustainable directions, and (c) involves planning for long-term (50–100 years in the future) outcomes (Hardoy et al. 2014). In addition, these CC strategies can also be linked to relevant biodiversity and conservation activities in the Yucatán Peninsula.

SUMMARY

This chapter has described the institutional framework for coastal management in the Yucatán Peninsula. It also provides a general overview of ICZM and how parts of it are currently addressed in Mexico. A key conclusion of the chapter is that

ICZM is a potentially demanding process that requires adequate information and strong institutions. It calls for focusing of efforts to targeted issues, and improving the information base on which decisions are made. Subsequent chapters in this report relate to geomorphology, selected social and economic dimensions of relevance in the Yucatán Peninsula, and potential reforms and enhancements to the EIA process: these all act as a bridge to some of the more detailed policy options and approaches that inform the conclusions presented in chapter 8.

NOTES

1. See http://glossary.eea.europa.eu/terminology/concept_html?term=ICZM (accessed December 2017).
2. See World Bank India Integrated Coastal Zone Management Project. http://www.world bank.org/projects/P097985/integrated-coastal-zone-management?lang=en.
3. SEMARNAT's website states that CIMARES has not met since 2012. http://www.semarnat .gob.mx/temas/ordenamiento-ecologico/historico-cimares/antecedentes. However, newspapers report on a meeting that took place in December 2015. See http://www.eluni versal.com.mx/articulo/nacion/sociedad/2015/12/17/recibe-titular-de-marina-presiden cia-de-cimares.
4. http://www.semarnat.gob.mx/sites/default/files/documentos/ordenamiento/decretados _20150617.jpg.

REFERENCES

Cicin-Sain, B., and S. Belfiore. 2005. "Linking Marine Protected Areas to Integrated Coastal and Ocean Management: A Review of Theory and Practice. *Ocean & Coastal Management* 48: 847–68.

CIMARES (Intersecretarial Commission for the Sustainable Management of Seas and Coasts). 2012. *Política nacional de mares y costas de México: Gestión integral de las regiones más dinámicas del territorio nacional.* Mexico City: SEMARNAT. http://biblio.upmx.mx/textos/9895.pdf.

Creel, J. E. 2005. "Protected Areas and Coastal and Ocean Management in Mexico." *Ocean & Coastal Management* 48 (11): 1016–46.

Dietz, T., E. Ostrom, and P. C. Stern. 2003. "The Struggle to Govern the Commons." *Science* 302 (5652): 1907–12.

Garcia, S. M. 2003. *The Ecosystem Approach to Fisheries: Issues, Terminology, Principles, Institutional Foundations, Implementation and Outlook.* Rome: FAO.

Hardoy, J., I. Hernández, J. A. Pacheco, and G. Sierra. 2014. "Institutionalizing Climate Change Adaptation at Municipal and State Level in Chetumal and Quintana Roo, Mexico." *Environment and Urbanization* 26 (1): 69–85. doi: 10.1177/0956247813519053.

Hernández, L. E. V., I. P. Romero, L. A. Soto, and E. R. Arriaga. 2012. "Legal Framework for the Offshore Operations of the Mexican Oil Industry from a Systemic Environmental Perspective." *Ocean & Coastal Management* 58: 9–16.

INE (Instituto Nacional de Ecología). 2012. *10 Propuestas de mejora inmediata para el Ordenamiento Ecológico Territorial* (10 Proposals for Immediate Improvement for Territorial Ecological Planning). http://www.semarnat.gob.mx/sites/default/files/documentos /ordenamiento/10propuestas_mejora_oet_inecc.pdf.

IPCC (Intergovernmental Panel on Climate Change). 2007. "Chapter 6: Paleoclimate" (Jansen, E., J. Overpeck, K. R. Briffa, J.-C. Duplessy, F. Joos, V. Masson-Delmotte, D. Olago, B. Otto-Bliesner, W.R. Peltier, S. Rahmstorf, R. Ramesh, D. Raynaud, D. Rind, O. Solomina, R. Villalba and D. Zhang). In *Climate Change 2007: The Physical Science Basis. Contribution of Working Group I to the Fourth Assessment Report of the Intergovernmental Panel on Climate Change*, edited by S. Solomon, D. Qin, M. Manning, Z. Chen, M. Marquis, K.B. Averyt, M. Tignor and H.L. Miller. Cambridge, UK, and New York, NY: Cambridge University Press.

Kennedy, A. J. 1994. "Cumulative Effects Assessment in Canada: From Concept to Practice." Papers from the Fifteenth Symposium Held by the Alberta Society of Professional Biologists. Calgary, AB: Alberta Society of Professional Biologists.

Lambeck, K., and J. Chappell. 2001. "Sea Level Change through the Last Glacial Cycle." *Science* 292: 679–86.

Lindeboom, H. 2002. "The Coastal Zone: An Ecosystem under Pressure." In *Oceans 2020: Science, Trends, and the Challenge of Sustainability*, 49–84. Washington, DC: Island Press.

Maltby, E. 2003. *Using the Ecosystem Approach to Implement the Convention on Biological Diversity: Key Issues and Case Studies (No. 2)*. Gland, Switzerland: IUCN (International Union for Conservation of Nature).

Matishov, G. G., V. V. Denisov, and Y. E. Kirillova. 1998. "Role of a Procedure of Environment Impact Assessment (EIA) in Elaborating the Integrated Project of Managing the Barents Sea Coastal Zones." *Ocean & Coastal Management* 41 (2): 221–36.

Ortega-Rubio, A., C. A. Salinas-Zavala, D. Lluch-Cota, and E. Troyo-Diéguez. 2001. "A New Method to Determine the Level of the Environmental Impact Assessment Studies in Mexico." *Environmental Impact Assessment Review* 21 (1): 73–81.

Ortiz-Lozano, L., I. Espejel, A. Granados-Barba, and P. Arceo. 2007. "A Functional and Integrated Approach of Methods for the Management of Protected Marine Areas in the Mexican Coastal Zone." *Ocean & Coastal Management* 50 (5): 379–91.

Saturnino, H. M., J. N. Landers, F. P. Cardoso, N. H. Pereira, R. Derpsch, J. R. Marinho, J. R. Batmanian, and Ministerio da Ciencia e da Tecnologia, Instituto de Investigacao Cientifica Tropical, Lisboa. 2008. *Perspectives on Integrated Coastal Zone Management in South America*, edited by R. J. Neves, J. Baretta, and M. Mateus. Lisbon: IST Press.

UNEP/GPA (United Nations Environment Programme/Global Action Programme). 2006. *Ecosystem-Based Management: Markers for Assessing Progress*. Nairobi: UNEP.

UNSD (United Nations Sustainable Development). 1993. *Agenda 21*. United Nations Conference on Environment & Development, Rio de Janeiro, Brazil, June 3–14, 1992. https://sustainabledevelopment.un.org/content/documents/Agenda21.pdf.

Vidal, L., and L. Capurro Filograsso. 2008. "Quantitative Analysis of Natural Resource Regulations Leading to Coastal Ecosystems Sustainability: Mexico as a Case Study." *Journal of Coastal Research*: 876–89.

Victorian Coastal Council. 2014. *Victorian Coastal Strategy 2014*. Melbourne: The State of Victoria Department of Environment and Primary Industries. https://www.coastsandmarine.vic.gov.au/__data/assets/pdf_file/0025/405835/VCS_2014.pdf.

Waite, R., L. Burke, and E. Gray. 2014. *Coastal Capital: Ecosystem Valuation for Decision Making in the Caribbean*. Washington, DC: World Resources Institute. http://www.wri.org/publication/coastal-capital-guidebook.

World Bank. 1996. "Noordwijk Guidelines for Integrated Coastal Zone Management." Document presented at the World Coast Conference 1993, Noordwijk, Netherlands, November 1–5. Republished as J.C. Post and C. G. Lundin (eds.). 1996. "Guidelines for Integrated Coastal Zone Management." Environmentally Sustainable Development Studies and Monograph Series 9, World Bank, Washington, DC.

——. 2016a. *Sustainable Development: FAQ—Landscapes*. http://web.worldbank.org/WBSITE/EXTERNAL/TOPICS/EXTSDNET/0,,contentMDK:23216619~menuPK:64885113~pagePK:7278667~piPK:64911824~theSitePK:5929282,00.html#Q1 (accessed April 2016).

——. 2016b. *Forest Action Plan FY16–20*. http://www-wds.worldbank.org/external/default/WDSContentServer/WDSP/IB/2016/04/15/090224b08429db6a/1_0/Rendered/PDF/Forest0action0plan0FY16020.pdf (accessed April 2016).

Yáñez-Arancibia, A., and J. W. Day. 2004. "The Gulf of Mexico: Towards an Integration of Coastal Management with Large Marine Ecosystem Management." *Ocean & Coastal Management* 47 (11): 537–63.

Yáñez-Arancibia, A.; J. W. Day, and E. Reyes. 2013. "Understanding the Coastal Ecosystem-Based Management Approach in the Gulf of Mexico." In *Understanding and Predicting Change in the Coastal Ecosystems of the Northern Gulf of Mexico*, edited by J. C. Brock, J. A. Barras, and S. J. Williams, *Journal of Coastal Research* (63): 243–61.

3 Coastal Geomorphology and Climate Change Adaptation

JOHN PETHICK AND JACK RUITENBEEK

BRIEF DESCRIPTION OF OVERALL GEOMORPHOLOGY

The Yucatán Peninsula forms part of the larger Yucatán Platform, composed of carbonate sediments dating from the Cretaceous. These sediments have depths of 3–4 km and extend over the 200 km wide Campeche Shelf to the west and north, and a narrower shelf on the east. The shelf is bounded in the west by the Yucatán Escarpment and to the east by the Yucatán Channel, which marks the boundary between the Gulf of Mexico and the Caribbean Sea (Kjerfve 1994).

The entire coastal zone of the peninsula is one of outstanding natural resources and beauty, which has enabled its tourism industry to become a significant sector of Mexico's economy. Most of the tourist industry is focused on the coastal zone and its coastal reefs, shoreline beaches, and ecologically important lagoons. The Biosphere Reserves of Sian Ka'an in Quintana Roo, Ría Celestún in Yucatán, and Laguna de Terminos in Campeche reflect the national and international importance of the Yucatán Peninsula's coastal ecology. They also provide a range of habitats that is dependent upon its physical characteristics—a karstic platform with few rivers, low tidal range, and a series of barrier islands. However, these natural resources face increasing threats from external changes such as increases in sea level and hurricane frequency, and from the presence of coastal infrastructure and its associated extensive and uncoordinated coastal defenses.

The coastlines of the Yucatán Peninsula can be conveniently divided into three distinct geomorphic regions, coinciding with the administrative boundaries of the three states of Campeche, Quintana Roo, and Yucatán.

QUINTANA ROO

The coastal zone of Quintana Roo lies within the zone of the Caribbean Sea and is developed on a low relief, karstic platform. It has a surface veneer of lithified Pleistocene Aeolian sands, extending seawards as a narrow shelf between 400 m and 1,000 m wide, with a narrow intermittent fringing coral reef extending along the coast. A series of islands (Mujeres, Blanca, and Contoy) and barrier beaches enclosing lagoons (Nichupte, Chakmochuk, and Holbox) with fringing coral reefs forms the northeast coast. Landward from Islas Mujeres and Contoy, the seabed is characterized by extensive sand waves, between 5 and 6 meters thick, and composed of ooids and bioclastic debris carried northwards and focused into this area by the Yucatán Current (Harms, Choquette, and Brady 1978). The coastal sediments lie on a platform of lithified aeolian sands forming headlands such as Punta Nizuc and Punta Cancún, between which barrier beaches and tombolas have developed. South of Punta Nizuc, a narrow beach ridge forms a series of pocket beaches between successive aeolianite headlands; the barrier beach and lithified beach ridges enclose a tidal mangrove wetland (Loucks and Ward 2001). In the southern part of the region, the coastal fringe of coral reefs and barrier islands protects extensive coastal wetlands and lagoons (Ascencion and Chetumal), with mangrove forest fed by fresh water from the largely subterranean karstic river system. Sediment sources for the entire region appear to be confined to coral debris from the fringing reefs; however, erosion of the underlying aeolian deposits may contribute a minor fraction of the total input. South of Isla Blanca, the coast is typified by erosion of the beach sediments and to a lesser extent the underlying carbonate aeolianites. Tidal range is between 0.2 and 0.6 meters and winds are predominantly from the northeast. This means that net sediment transport in the northern section of this coast is northwards, but to the south of Punta Nizuc, this reverses to give a net southward drift. The implications of this sediment divide on the overall coastal behavior and its impact on human development of this coast are discussed below.

CAMPECHE

The coast of Campeche State forms the western coast of the Yucatán Peninsula and faces a broad submarine shelf extending to the Campeche Bank Reefs, a series of emergent platform reefs and submerged bank reefs. Average rainfall falls to less than 400 mm in the north of Campeche State. This, together with the karstic topography, means that, apart from the Rio Champoton, there are few surface rivers and fresh water discharges into the coastal zone in a series of springs.

The northwestern coast lies in the wave shadow of the dominant northeasterly waves that characterize the northern coast of the peninsula. As a result of this low energy regime, the nearshore to the north of Campeche City is composed of deposits of fine-grained, cohesive carbonate sediment, perhaps derived from the coral reefs that lie on the Campeche Shelf, and which mask the underlying limestone rock. The seaward margin of the coast supports mangrove vegetation backed by a wide saline plain, largely unvegetated, and which merges landward into a second mangrove belt. This section of the coast is undeveloped and is of high ecological value.

In the center, between Campeche City and Champoton, the limestone has been tectonically uplifted to form a cliff coastline, merging into a series of beach ridges formed from Pleistocene carbonate sands and gravels, lithified into beach rock. South of Champoton lies a wide depositional plain, probably of mid-Holocene age and with up to 40 ridges, reported by some authors (for example, Psuty 1965; Thom 1967) to be composed of mobile shell fragments, whose landward boundary is a fossil shore cut into the Pleistocene conglomerates. South of this zone, the coastal barrier island of Isla del Carmen encloses the Laguna de Terminos. The Real Inlet to the east and the Carmen inlet to the west are both dredged channels; although tidal range is small (0.5 m), substantial tidal deltas have formed at both entrances to the lagoon, with a flood tide delta on the Real Inlet and an ebb tide delta at the Carmen Inlet (David and Kjerfve 1998). The seaward shoreline of the island is experiencing rapid erosion, in particular during hurricanes when sediment overwash is a major problem to settlement and roads.

YUCATÁN

The northern coast of the Yucatán Peninsula lies within the Gulf of Mexico oceanographic province. The coast fronts a wide (200 km) submarine shelf with a slope of 1:1,000 extending north to the Campeche and Alacran Reefs. Tides are mixed, with a diurnal dominance and a tidal range of between 0.1 and 0.8 meters. Waves are dominantly from the northeast, but veering to southeast, towards the Quintana Roo coast (Appendini et al. 2012; Ward and Brady 1973). The coastal zone is a flat, highly permeable, karstic plain with no surface rivers, but with a series of coastal lagoons landward of a 200 km long line of barrier islands formed of multiple beach ridges developed during the Holocene. These lagoons are tidal, but receive fresh water from groundwater springs or direct runoff from bordering mangroves during the rainy season (June to October). The western coast has been extensively urbanized for tourism and summer home residents (Meyer-Arendt 1991). These coastal properties are exceptionally vulnerable to wave damage, flooding, and sand inundation. Despite the high rainfall (1,500 mm/year), water supply and sewage disposal is a major problem in this permeable, karstic area.

The barrier beaches extending along the coast are formed of carbonate sands probably derived from the extensive sand-wave deposits that accumulate in the lee of Islas Mujeres and Contoy, and which are transported westward towards Holbox and the Yucatán coast by wave-driven currents. Longshore transport along the northern coast is dominantly east to west, with rates estimated at between 20,000 m^3 a^{-1} and 70,000 m^3 a^{-1} (Appendini et al. 2012). This relatively low rate reflects the low wave energy propagated across the wide shelf.

The successive beach ridges clearly show the accretionary nature of the coast; yet, despite this indication of a Holocene history of deposition, the coast is now characterized by erosion at rates averaging between 1 and 2 meters per year.

SUMMARY OF COASTAL ISSUES IMPORTANT FOR THE ECONOMY

Sea level rise

Sea level rise, both existing and predicted, is likely to be the major factor affecting Yucatán coastal behavior over the next few decades. Landward migration of the barrier beaches due to existing sea level rise, exacerbated by accelerated eustatic sea level rise and local seasonal fluctuations, both due to global warming, will affect all shoreline properties. Sand inundation of backshore properties will also occur as barriers roll over. Shore defenses to combat the erosion, already deployed by local residents, will lead to increased erosion downdrift (Appendini et al. 2012).

A preliminary examination of the tide gauge records from Progreso and Ciudad de Carmen, undertaken for this study, suggests a relative sea level rise over the past few decades of between 3 and 5 mm per year. This existing rise in sea level may be in addition to that predicted to occur because of global warming. Current IPCC predictions (Church et al. 2013) under a low emission scenario (that is, RCP 2.6) are for a total rise in sea level of 0.26 m by 2100 and 0.95 m for a worst-case scenario (that is, RCP 8.5). However, many authorities consider that this underestimates the threat and suggest that eustatic sea level will rise by between 0.5 and 2.0 m (Nicholls et al. 2011). This, together with the existing rate of 3–5 mm per year on the Yucatán coast, would mean a total sea level rise of between 0.77 m and 2.45 m by the end of the century. In addition, the predicted rise in ocean temperatures due to global warming may increase the existing seasonal fluctuation in water levels along this coast, currently shown by the Progreso tide gauge record to be around 300 mm. Hurricane frequency and intensity, already increasing, may accelerate further. Such increases in sea level and storm events would force the barrier beaches landwards onto the mainland and lead to the loss of the lagoons and other coastal habitats—reducing their potential for human usage (Blum et al. 2002).

Increased hurricane frequency

The increase in hurricane frequency and intensity associated with global warming may accelerate the problems caused by sea level rise (Webster et al. 2005). As hurricane frequency increases, recovery from hurricane damage, both to the shoreline and to the fringing reef systems, will be incomplete between successive events, leading to progressive deterioration of the systems.

It can be argued that the general morphology of the Yucatán coast is presently adjusted to medium-frequency, medium-magnitude storms such as the winter northerly storms (nortes), rather than the low-frequency, high-magnitude hurricanes. Hurricane damage to coral reefs, beaches, and dunes—such as that produced by Gilbert in 1988 and by Wilma in 2005—can be severe, but these natural coastal systems recover from such impacts and resume their former function and form before the next hurricane event, which occur once every decade, on average. In addition, hurricanes can produce some benefits to the natural coastal system such as the production of coral debris. Those fragments act as an essential sediment input to coastal sediment cells and which therefore accelerates the recovery process (Conner et al. 1989). The predicted increase in hurricane frequency and intensity equates to an increase in net hurricane power, and, thus, in hurricanes' destructive potential so that coastal systems, both natural and human, will be forced to adjust to this new environment control (Emmanuel 2005).

Shoreline erosion

Coastal erosion is now seen as a major issue for the social and economic development of all three coastal states on the Yucatán Peninsula. Rates of erosion vary according to the area under review. For example, Meyer-Arendt (1991) reports rates of 0.6 m per year at Progreso, while Gonzalez-Leija et al.

(2013) reported 15 m per year at Cancún. In contrast, Diez (2009), working on the Cancún shore, reports a 34 m retreat in the period 1984–2004, a rate of 1.7 m per year. Gutierrez-Estrada, Castro-Del Rio, and Galaviz-Solis (1988) calculated an average erosion rate 1.8 m per year for the north Yucatán coast over a 110-year period. It is important to recognize that most erosion records provided in the literature are for periods commencing at least 50, and in some case 100, years ago, indicating that shore erosion on the Yucatán is not a recent phenomenon.

The explanations often advanced for this widespread erosion are (a) sea level rise due to global warming, and (b) human interference in the coastal system. Neither explanation provides an adequate reason for the observed erosion rates. Future sea level rise may result in substantial coastal recession. However, as shown by the Progreso tide gauge, sea level rise over the past 50 years has totaled 250 mm, which it is unlikely to account for the widespread loss of beach sands and associated coastal recession. It is possible that an increase in water depth of 250 mm could drown out sand waves on the seabed, lifting the wave base to prevent sand transport to the shore, but such a process again is unlikely to account for widespread erosion rates of 1–2 m per year. Human interference in the form of hard structures built to combat erosion necessarily postdates the erosion process and therefore cannot be responsible for its initiation, although it may exacerbate rather than reduce erosion rates. Indeed, reported erosion rates commencing at least 100 years ago support the conclusion that the process began before extensive human development of this coast.

Coastal erosion is a response to reduction in sediment supply to the coastal system, so that potential sediment transport rates by wave-driven currents can only be met by erosion of existing sediments within the system. Sediment sources for the Yucatán coastal system are primarily the modern coral reefs, although some inputs may derive from erosion of fossil carbonate sands. Degradation of the coral reef systems, partly due to global warming (for example, bleaching, increased frequency of hurricane damage) and partly due to anthropogenic impacts (for example, pollution) will result in a reduction of carbonate sediment available for beach replenishment.

Urbanization of the shoreline

Although Mayan culture avoided coastal locations, most probably in response to the volatile nature of the region, the necessity for port locations in the 19th century, and the more recent development of domestic shoreline homes in Yucatán and commercial tourism in Quintana Roo have led to urbanization of the coast and exposure of this infrastructure to extreme events.

Meyer-Arendt (1991) has referred to the "recreational frontier" of small domestic houses on the Yucatán coast centered on Progreso and expanding eastwards, engulfing small fishing villages. In Quintana Roo, Torres and Momsen (2005) have described the development by the Mexican government of an "isolated tropical forest enclave" at Cancún to initiate the highly successful economic development strategy of Planned Tourism Development that has now enveloped the shoreline of the Nichupte lagoon with hotel complexes (Bezaury et al. 1998). In contrast, the coast of Campeche remains largely undeveloped, although there is increasing pressure for both domestic and commercial recreational use, particularly in the southern coastal zone (Rivera-Arriaga and Villalobos-Zapata 2005).

The perceived necessity of a shoreline location for such development, both domestic and commercial, has largely ignored the inherent dangers of the coast, threats that include floods and direct hurricane damage as well as shoreline erosion. In many cases, if not most, the development has extended to the upper shoreline, ignoring the 20 m federal maritime zone, so that former mobile beach ridges and sand dunes have been engulfed.

The results of this development have been twofold. First, natural coastal hazards have affected socioeconomic development, which includes the construction of largely uncoordinated coastal defense systems and, more significantly, domestic investment. Meyer-Arendt (1991), for example, concluded that investment in international tourism development slowed down after the 1988 hurricane. Impacts of hurricanes in the past, coupled with predictions of increased storm frequency and rising sea levels in the future have prompted more short-term investment with negative impacts on both the urban and natural environment.

Second, the impact of shoreline urbanization on the natural environment has been to decrease the resilience of the shore to natural hazards and to increase the threats from both erosion and flooding. The envelopment of mobile dunes and barrier beaches by urban infrastructure and hard coastal defenses prevents their adjustment to environment changes. Erosion of a shoreline is, in almost all cases, a negative feedback response to decreased sediment supply so that the coastline changes its orientation with respect to dominant waves, and a lower transport rate is produced, thus reducing and eventually eliminating erosion. Urbanized coasts are unable to respond in this way so that potential sediment transport rates remain high and erosion of the seabed proceeds until shoreline defenses are undermined and collapse.

Low elevation coasts, such as those of the Yucatán Peninsula, have natural flood defenses in the form of barrier beaches, which migrate landward as sea level rises so maintaining their standard of protection. The virtual petrification of these former mobile barriers by urbanization means that no such migration can take place so that barriers will be overtopped by rising sea levels rather than move landwards and upwards.

CURRENT ACTIVITIES FOR EROSION MANAGEMENT

The response of most coastal managers to erosion is to provide shore defenses, which, as shown above, can reduce the resilience of the coast to natural hazards and in some cases can actually increase erosion rates. The north Yucatán coast provides many examples of such management problems, where construction of "espigones" (groins) in the 20th century resulted in accelerated erosion downdrift. There are three major types of response to erosion currently used in Yucatán: hard defenses, beach nourishment, and artificial reefs.

Hard defenses (groins, seawalls)

The most common response to coastal erosion on the Yucatán Peninsula, as elsewhere in the world, is to construct hard defenses in the form of groins and seawalls.

Meyer-Arendt (1991) describes the response to erosion on the north Yucatán coast as driven by individual hurricane events, coupled with coastal construction works. The 1944 hurricane, for example, exacerbated erosion already in progress along the Progreso shore, following the development of the harbor there. This led to a government initiative in 1964 to build a series of rock and timber groins (espigones); the impact of these espigones, coupled with further harbor development, including dredging of the harbor navigation channel, resulted in increased downdrift erosion. The response was a widespread and unauthorized construction of espigones by beachfront property owners, without permits, and encroaching on the 20 m federal maritime zone. Over 150 espigones were initially constructed in this way, but by 1980, it became obvious that these actually accelerated downdrift erosion and subsequently their construction was formally banned. Hurricane Juan in 1985 prompted a new phase of defense construction by local property owners, this time in the form of seawalls, usually of the "staircase" design, and by 1987, almost 20 percent of frontage properties were so "protected." Hurricane Gilbert (1988) caused extensive damage to these new constructions by undermining their foundations; most properties fronting the sea were destroyed and sediment overwash inundated those located further landward. Few of these properties were insured.

In Cancún, a similar set of responses to hurricane events has taken place but here properties, mostly owned by national and international corporations, are insured. Thus, following Hurricane Gilbert in 1988, extensive repair of damaged frontage hotels and business properties took place. Defenses, mainly in the form of sea walls, but including riprap barriers, were constructed, but loss of beach material continued. This prompted a beach nourishment program as detailed below.

Beach nourishment

Beach nourishment appears to be the presently favored approach to coastal defense. Programs recently implemented or currently in progress include the 3 million cubic meter recharge at Cancún, recirculation of dredged sediment from navigation channels along the north Yucatán coast and a proposed recharge of beaches protected by artificial reef for a new hotel complex at San Miguelito, Quintana Roo (Diez et al. 2009).

The critical factor in each of these recharge schemes is the extraction area for the recharge sand. In such schemes, sediment should normally be extracted from the downdrift side of the recharge site so that sand is carried back to the extraction site and a circulatory system is set up. However, in some cases, such as those involving harbor or navigation dredging, dredged sediment should be sidecast in the direction of drift rather than against it so that recharge acts as a sediment-bypass process. Therefore, sediment recharge requires careful consideration of the sediment transport pathways prior to sediment extraction; in many cases, no such analysis is provided, leading to progressive deterioration of the coastal system. A brief discussion of the three areas of recharge on the Yucatán Peninsula listed above will amplify this point.

(a) In the case of the north Yucatán recharge program, although direct extraction is from beach deposits, some of these deposits are temporary stores for dredged arisings from navigation channels. This means that the process of recharge is in effect harbor bypassing. Sediment transport of this coast is east to west so that dredged arising should be moved in that direction.

(b) The scheme for recharge at San Miguelito, between Puerto Morelos and Playa del Carmen on the Quintana Roo coast, proposes extraction from a sand bank inshore of a local coral reef immediately north of the recharge site. This would short-circuit the net sediment transport pathway on this coast, which is from north to south, leading to accelerated erosion north of the recharge site and obviating any benefit to the site itself.

(c) The Cancún recharge scheme is in a complex area of sediment transport lying across a sediment divide. Extraction was from the Mujeres Bay sand banks, an area of extensive sand waves described above. Approximately 3×10^6 m³ of sand was extracted from this source and placed on the shore between Punta Cancún and Punta Nizuc, as reported by Diez et al. (2009), who note that relatively little information is available on the subsequent behavior of the coast after recharge. Discussion of the probable sediment transport pathways for this area was given above, where it was noted that a major sediment divergence occurs along this section of the coast. Thus, movement of the recharge sediment is likely to move either north or south, depending on the position of the recharge in relation to the divergence zone. If the recharge lies on the southern side of the divergence, then sediment transport would be south towards the eroding beaches between Puerto Morelos and Tulum. If, on the other hand, the recharge is to the north of the divergence, then sediment transport will be northwards to the already sediment-rich beaches of north Quintana Roo.

Artificial reefs

There is a growing interest in the deployment of artificial reefs designed for coastal defense around the world and a few such schemes have been advocated for the Yucatán Peninsula, although there are no published accounts of these. One such scheme is that on the mid-Quintana Roo coast at San Miguelito, where an artificial concrete reef is proposed to protect an artificially recharged beach. The artificial reef would be located between the natural fringing coral reef and the shore. The scheme is intended to reduce wave energy at the beach to reduce erosion rates, which presently average 1 m per year. However, one effect of the artificial reef may be the disruption of sediment inputs (that is, coral debris), from natural reef to shore. As noted above, coral debris constitutes one of the main sediment inputs to this sediment cell and any reduction in this input will be critical. A decrease in sediment supply to the near-shore here would result in accelerated sediment transport along the near-shore, perhaps accelerating beach erosion.

MAJOR COASTAL PROCESSES THAT DEFINE THE PENINSULA

The geomorphology of the coast of the Yucatán Peninsula has not received detailed attention in the scientific literature. Several papers and books deal with the geology of the area (for example, Perry et al. 2003; Ward, Weidie, and Back 1985) and there is a substantial literature on the ecology of the coast (see, for example, Bezaury et al. 1998), but few authors have focused on the dynamics of sediment and coastal morphology. Notable exceptions are the work of Appendini et al. (2012), Diez et al. (2008), and Diez et al. (2009). Appendini et al. (2012) provide a detailed analysis of sediment transport along the coast of northern Yucatán, while Diez et al. (2009) focus on the Quintana Roo coast between Cancún and Tumul. Nevertheless, there are no published accounts of the large-scale geomorphology of the peninsula.

One problem facing any such investigation is the lack of primary data on coastal energy and materials. There are no wave data for the area and only two tide gauges: at Progreso and Carmen. Studies of beach sediment are restricted to granulometry and chemistry (for example, Phleger and Ayala-Castanares 1971) and there have been no attempts to identify beach sand sources or sinks.

As a result, both of this lack of data and the paucity of published accounts, any summary given here must be in the form of a first approximation designed to encourage further research, rather than provide a secure foundation.

SEDIMENT CELLS ON THE YUCATÁN PENINSULA

One of the major tasks of a coastal management process is to identify sediment cells along the coast. The sediment cell is a stretch of coast between boundaries that partly or wholly contain sediment movement. Any development within the sediment cell will therefore have a minimal impact on areas outside its boundaries. Thus, the sediment cell provides a self-contained area for coastal planning. Within a sediment cell, the impacts of development will be contained and can often be mitigated, secure in the knowledge that neighboring regions will be unaffected.

The identification of sediment cells is an iterative process, whereby an initial approximate definition is subsequently refined as additional data is acquired. It is also important to ensure that the major cells are identified into which minor sub-cells are nested. Thus, for example, Vanegas, Serratos, and Casarin (2013) identified 16 sub-cells on the Campeche coast south of Ciudad de Campeche, all of which may be subsumed within single primary cells.

A preliminary attempt at identification of the primary sediment cells on the Yucatán Peninsula has been undertaken as part of this analytical work. Five primary cells have been defined (map 3.1). A short review of the process involved in identification of each cell is given below.

Preliminary definition of sediment cells for the Yucatán Peninsula

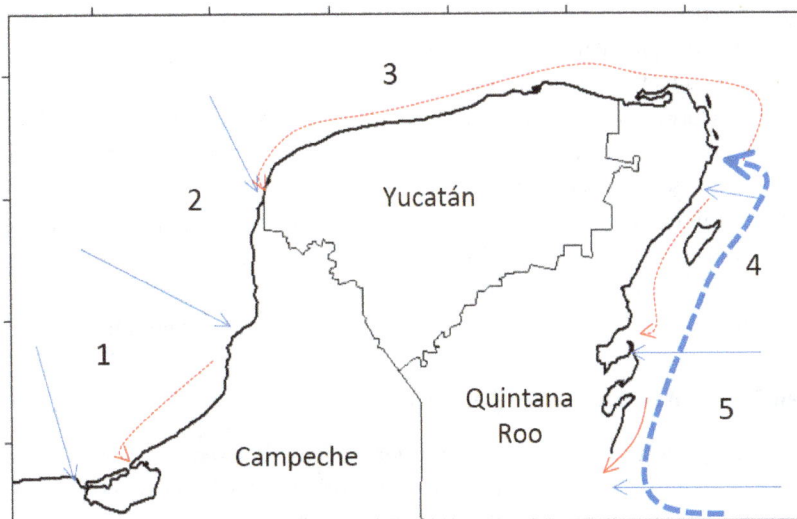

Note: Red arrows indicate tentative sediment pathways and direction; blue dashed arrow indicates the Yucatán current; blue straight arrows indicate the boundaries of the preliminary sediment cells.

Cell 1: Southern Campeche

This sediment cell occupies the eastern section of the Gulf of Campeche, with the western half extending across Tabasco and into Veracruz. The southern shore of the cell between Ciudad del Carmen and Chinking is a wide sedimentary plain composed of a series of beach ridges, while the northern shores between Ciudad del Carmen and Champoton are devoid of superficial sediment. There are no coral reefs apart from the distant Campeche and Alacran reefs. The cell therefore presents a problem in that there appears to be no sediment source for the large volume of sediment contained in the beach ridges of the southern shore.

Several authors (for example, Castillo et al. 1991; Psuty 1965) have commented that the ridges are composed of shell fragments rather than the quartz sand that forms a similar ridge within Tabasco State, but no direct sedimentological evidence for this was provided and it may be that only the modern beach is formed from shells. However, if the beach is formed from molluscan shell fragments, then the source must be from the nearshore seabed and it is probable that the series of beach ridges was formed during extreme events such as "nortes" and hurricanes, which winnow the low-density shell material from the nearshore seabed and transport onto the upper shore. If this hypothesis is accepted, then the erosion of the shoreline between Champoton and Ciudad del Carmen may be due to a decrease in productivity of mollusks here, perhaps due to overfishing or to pollution. Nevertheless, there are several examples where it is clear that direct human intervention has resulted in local erosion. One example of this is the erosion of the foreshore of Carmen Island, where the recent dredging of Real Inlet into Laguna de Terminos resulted in the diversion of shell sands into the lagoon forming extensive islands there, while the loss of sediment on the downdrift side of the inlet has caused erosion of the Isla de Carmen shore.

Cell 2: Northern Campeche

The Campeche coast between Ciudad de Campeche and Celestun lies in the wave shadow of the dominant northeasterly waves that characterize the northern coast of the peninsula. As a result, this area is characterized by a low energy regime so that the nearshore is composed of deposits of fine-grained carbonate muds, derived partly from the coral reefs that lie on the Campeche Shelf, and partly from in situ vegetation. The seaward margin of the coast supports mangrove vegetation backed by a wide saline plain, largely unvegetated, and which merges landward into a second mangrove belt. This section of the coast is undeveloped and is of high ecological value.

Since this cell is characterized by fine-grained sediment, it cannot be treated in the same way as those cells formed in sand-sized material. This is because ocean currents transport fine-grained sediments in suspension over long distances; consequently, boundaries to sediment pathways are not relevant.

Cell 3: Yucatán to North Quintana Roo

Preliminary observations of satellite imagery suggest that a continuous sediment pathway, identified on satellite imagery by major sand waves, exists between Isla Contoy in Quintana Roo and Celestun in Yucatán. This is supported by the work of Appendini et al. (2012), which provides modeled predictions of potential transport pathways and rates on this shore. Although Appendini et al. (2012) do not speculate on the sediment's source, it is likely to be the extensive sand-wave field extending from Isla Mujeres to Isla Contoy in Quintana Roo. Harms, Choquette, and Brady (1978) described this field and recent (2012) satellite imagery showed it. Appendini et al. (2012) predict that the net western potential sediment transport rates on this coast are in the region of 20,000–70,000 m³ per year.

Yucatán's northern coast is characterized by an almost continuous barrier beach backed by a sequence of beach ridges and sand dunes, as well as numerous lagoons, which appear to represent sediment stores for any excess sands transported alongshore and thus balancing the sediment budget. These sediment stores culminate in the barrier beach and lagoon at Celestun, an area that satellite imagery shows as accreting between 2004 and 2013, perhaps indicating an overall positive sediment budget for this primary cell.

The sand-wave field in northern Quintana Roo extends over an area of approximately 40 km², which, assuming an average thickness of 5 m, represents a total sand store of over 200×10^6 m³: sufficient to supply two millennia of longshore transport along the Yucatán coast. This, together with the satellite imagery showing sand waves along the entire coastal zone of Yucatán and the accretion at Celestun, suggests that there is no sediment deficit on this coast.

If this is a correct assumption then the erosion rates observed along this coast cannot be explained by changes in environmental conditions and it may be therefore that the observed erosion is due to human interference in the sediment transport pathways. The construction of the pier at Progreso, together with the dredging of the harbor channel, resulted in rapid downdrift erosion and has been often quoted as an example of the negative impacts of coastal construction (for example, Meyer-Arendt 1991). Numerous other examples of a similar cause-effect process can be seen to the east of Progreso (such as at Chicxulub and Telchac).

However, an alternative hypothesis may be proposed for this cell, based on observations of the sequence of beach ridges that occur along the north Yucatán coast. The sequence at Ría Lagartos, for example, shows approximately 50 beach ridges whose orientation with respect to the modern shoreline swings clockwise as they become younger. Erosion of the present-day shore has truncated the most-modern ridges at their eastern extremities. The orientation of a shoreline with respect to dominant wave direction is an indication of the strength of the longshore current and a clockwise swing on this coast indicates a decrease in the current velocities over time. The implication is that sediment transport along this coast has gradually declined over the Holocene and that, more recently, this decline has resulted in a negative sediment budget in which potential sediment transport is not met by supply, resulting in erosion of the foreshore.

These alternative hypotheses are clearly incompatible, with one suggesting a positive sediment budget and only human induced local erosion, while the other proposing a long-term decline in sediment supply terminating in a negative budget today. Both hypotheses are considered here as an example of the process by which behavioral models are advanced for individual sediment cells—the basic methodology leading to shoreline management planning. The next stage should be the acquisition of a detailed database that will allow rigorous testing of such behavioral models and thus, to inform the management process.

Cell 4: Northern Quintana Roo

As a first approximation, it is proposed here that Cell 4 extends from a divergent sediment boundary in the north to Punta Allen at the mouth of Ascension Lagoon in the south. Sediment inputs across the northern boundary are from the seabed sediment store between Puerto Morelos and Punta Cancún. Additional sediment input along the shore is coral debris from the fringing reefs that front this coast. The net sediment pathway along the coast is southward, although there is a strong cross-shore sediment movement as noted by Diez et al. (2009). This may mean that sediment is moved from the beach to the deeper water offshore where it moves into the northward-moving Yucatán Current (for example Kjerfve 1994). It is proposed that this northerly, high-velocity current moves the cross-shore sediment northward where it is deposited in the seabed store in the lee of Isla Mujeres and Contoy as described above (map 3.1). The remaining sediment inshore of the reefs continues south to Punta Allen where it is carried into Ascension Lagoon and deposited in a sediment sink (that is, removed from further coastal processes).

The northern boundary of this cell cannot be precisely defined given the available information, but lies between Puerto Morelos and Cancún. Gonzalez-Leija et al. (2013) proposed that a divergent sediment divide exists between Punta Cancún and Punta Nizuc, and this is consistent with morphological evidence that shows a major change in coastal orientation at Cancún. Although wave data is not available for this area, Appendini at al. (2012) provide a wave rose for a point 50 km east of Cancún, based on hind-cast modeling, which shows that the dominant waves here are southeasterly. Although wave refraction would modify the wave approach angle at the shore, the net sediment transport pathway will be northwards north of Cancún, while the pathway will be southward south of Cancún. The exact location of such a divide will vary according to wave conditions at any given moment, but in general, this describes a divergent sediment boundary located between Punta Cancún and Puerto Morelos.

A divergent sediment boundary implies either that sediment is input to the divide from offshore, or that sediment is eroded from the shore to feed the opposing sediment pathways. In this case, both the options may apply: the sediment store in the straits between Isla Mujeres/Contoy and the mainland has been described above and several authors have documented the erosion of the shoreline along the Cancún shore.

Cell 5: Southern Quintana Roo

Cell 5 is defined here as extending from Puerto Madero at the mouth of Espiritu Santo Lagoon to Canjero Cay at the mouth of the Chetumal Lagoon. This sediment cell is characterized by a thin sand veneer on intertidal beaches, mainly contained within pocket bays defined by a series of minor headlands formed from the underlying aeolianites. Sediment inputs appear to be restricted to coral debris from the fringing reefs. Net sediment movement is southerly, but with the strong cross-shore component noted above for Cell 4. During storm events, beach sediment moves seaward across the shore (drawdown) and meets the northward-moving Yucatán Current. It is possible therefore that some sediment from Cell 5 enters into the outer pathway of the circulatory system of Cell 4, thus the sediment from both cells moves north with the Yucatán Current and is redeposited in the lee of Isla Contoy. However, the presence of the three major sediment sink areas (Ascension, Espiritu Santo and Chetumal lagoons) between Cell 4 and Cell 5 acts as a receptor for the southward moving inner pathway and prevents the completion of a full circulation pathway linking the two cells.

MANAGEMENT OF THE COASTAL AND MARINE AREAS

Shoreline management

Shoreline Management is the physical management of the shore to reduce the impact of natural hazards, such as flooding and erosion, but also to mitigate the physical impact of human intervention in the coastal system. Its overall objective is a self-sustaining shore system: resilient and not requiring human maintenance. Therefore, shoreline management constitutes one component of the larger program integrated coastal zone management (ICZM); it may be thought of as providing an interface between coastal science and coastal management. The process of shoreline management includes production of a Shoreline Management Plan (SMP), designed to evaluate the behavior of a coast, both in response to environmental and human impacts, and to use this information to inform the economic, social and environmental plans for the coast. In this sense, the SMP offers information to the ICZM planners; thus, it must aim for efficient communication of relevant coastal science to ICZM planners.

Shoreline management plans: Structure and content

A SMP sets out how the coast should best be managed in the future. It is

- An account of the past and predicted future behavior of a stretch of coastline, normally defined as a sediment cell
- A large scale assessment of the risks for people and property associated with coastal processes within the SMP area and
- Designed to inform a policy framework that sustainably reduces risks to people and to the developed, historic, and natural environments—a policy framework that is central to the ICZM process.

SMPs set out the approach to achieve long-term sustainability of coastal risk management for a specific stretch of coast. Their aim is to provide the basis for sustainable shoreline management policies over the next 100 years within a natural process unit (sediment cell or sub-cell). The stretch of coast that an SMP covers includes one or more sediment cells and will typically include a number of communities and land uses, and a series of different physical features and coastal defenses.

The process of SMP development includes five main tasks:

1) Definition of sediment cells as the basic unit for coastal zone management,
2) Collation of a coastal database designed to support the science within the SMP,
3) Development of conceptual (or behavioral) models for each sediment cell,
4) Evaluation of societal demands on the coast, and
5) Reconciliation of scientific and societal demands within the SMP framework.

Table 3.1 shows the content of the final SMP. It describes the physical processes of the coast, reviews its present and anticipated land use, and outlines policies that could result in long-term sustainable use. Finally, after

TABLE 3.1 Structure of the sediment management plan

SECTION	CONTENT
Coastal behavior	Outline of hindcast and forecast geomorphological behavior models of the coast within each sediment cell boundary
Prediction of future coastal behavior	Prediction of future change in large-scale morphology, flooding, and erosion risks; normally for the next 100 years
Land use	Outline of existing coastal zone usage: agriculture, urban, ports, industry, ecological, heritage, and so forth
Coastal management objectives	Summary of known objectives for the coastal zone (development of tourism and ports, industry, urbanization, and so forth)
Policy development	Outline of policies that would allow long-term sustainable development of the coast. A series of policy units may be defined along the coast within which each policy may be applied. These may not necessarily coincide with the sediment cell boundaries. Policies may include coastal defense provision, managed retreat from coastal hazard zones, or zero development.
Preferred policy selection	Selection of preferred policy for each policy unit based on economic, social, technical, and environmental criteria

consultation with coastal user groups, the SMP should report on a preferred option for shoreline management that reconciles both its natural processes and the human uses.

Sediment cells

The sediment cell is a stretch of coast between boundaries that partly or wholly contain sediment movement. It is the basic functional unit of the coast. It acts as a self-contained unit so that any development within the sediment cell will have a minimal impact on areas outside its boundaries. Within its boundaries, coastal processes act as a coherent, integrated system. An understanding of the way that this system functions allows identification of the impacts of development or management and identification of ways to take action to mitigate such impacts.

In order to define the boundaries of a coastal sediment cell, it is necessary to understand the way in which it functions. This is an iterative process in which a first approximation of the sediment cell boundaries is made based on whatever information is available, followed by a detailed review of the coastal processes within this approximation, based on a more comprehensive database, which may lead to boundary adjustment.

Conceptual models

Conceptual or behavioral geomorphological models are currently seen as an essential stage in managing a coastal area and they form the basis for the SMP. A conceptual model is a summary of the overall functioning of the coastal system within sediment cell boundaries. It considers the historic evolution of the coast, its present day processes and morphology and, crucially, attempts to predict future changes. Conceptual models are high-level models that encompass rather than replace more-specific quantitative models. Thus, a conceptual model may suggest scenarios that can be tested using hydrodynamic models.

A critical stage in the development of the conceptual model is the development of a sediment budget. Information from a variety of sources, both secondary and primary, is used to build up a composite map of sediment sources, sinks, stores, and pathways. This in turn allows a more precise definition of the sediment cell boundaries as part of the iterative process mentioned above. Since predicting future coastal change is the end product of the study, the changes in wave or tidal energy, the sources and sinks for sediment, and human inhibition of sediment movement all contribute to coastal morphological change and form the basis for the conceptual model. Thus, the conceptual, modeling stage of the SMP must depend on the collation of an adequate database, whose principal attributes are outlined below.

The Yucatán Peninsula database

A key component of the development of an SMP should be the collection, storage, and retrieval of coastal data that can be used to develop the conceptual models of the coast. Data should be acquired from both primary and secondary (that is, existing) sources, with a bias towards secondary data to reduce both costs and time; but in many cases secondary data sources are either lacking or inadequate.

The existing database for the Yucatán Peninsula is not considered adequate to support any detailed shoreline management. The limited data available focus on local issues at scales significantly smaller than those of the sediment cells outlined above. This means that management tends to rely on reducing local impacts, rather than seeking general causes of coastal problems. The lack of any data on waves, tides, currents, bathymetry, and shoreline topography, and the minimal data on sea level rise, are a major impediment to effective shoreline management. Urgent attention must be given to redress this situation.

Primary data

Primary data inputs should be kept to a minimum in view of the timing, cost, and applicability of such data. Detailed primary data obtained from field survey is normally obtained to test a specific hypothesis. Such hypotheses emerge only in the secondary stages of any investigation, as the initial aim of this study is to generate general behavioral models rather than investigate specific causal hypotheses. Thus, primary data collection must be concerned with obtaining general background information. There are four categories of coastal data required at this stage:

1) Coastal energy
2) Coastal morphology
3) Coastal sediments and
4) Coastal ecology.

The measurement of these components should form part of a general monitoring or surveillance system for the Yucatán coast. This should ideally be organized on an interstate basis, perhaps by federal agencies, to avoid unnecessary duplication and to ensure a comprehensive approach.

Table 3.2 summarizes the key attributes of each category that should be included in the basic monitoring system. It is essential that each attribute is considered both as a spatial and a temporal variable, since many, if not most, natural

TABLE 3.2 Categories for primary data collection

CATEGORY	ATTRIBUTES	METHOD
Energy	Waves	Waverider buoys
	Tides	Tide gauges
	Sea level	Tide gauges
Morphology	Intertidal	GPS
	Bathymetry	Echo sounder
	Supratidal	Remote sensing
Sediments	Clastic (muds)	Field samples. Granulometry and chemical analysis
	Nonclastic (sands, gravels)	Field samples/remote sensing. Granulometry/chemical analysis
Ecology	Mangroves, marshes, sand dunes, lagoons, corals, and seagrass beds	Remote sensing mapping (satellite/aerial photo)

TABLE 3.3 Attributes of secondary data collection

CATEGORY	ATTRIBUTES
Maps	Historical maps and charts
Charts	Port Authority bathymetric charts, Mexican naval charts
Satellite imagery	Obtained, for example, from NOAA
Aerial photographs	Obtained, for example, from INEGI
Literature review	Limited scientific literature exists. Advice on gray literature from, for example, Instituto de Ingeniería, Universidad Nacional Autónoma de México
Human impacts	Inventory and mapping of all potential human impacts on the coast

Note: NOAA = National Oceanic and Atmospheric Administration; INEGI = Instituto Nacional de Estadística y Geografía.

processes have return intervals measured in years or even decades; for this reason, all monitoring should be designed to be a continuous process.

The location, density, periodicity, and extent of primary data collection are matters for detailed planning. An initial proposal might be to base surveillance systems within each of the preliminary sediment cells defined above. Within each sediment cell, each of the attributes shown in table 3.2 should be monitored.

Secondary data

Secondary data, despite the term "secondary", are of central importance. Ideally, secondary data should be obtained and reviewed before primary field data collection is planned so that the design of the primary data monitoring system might be based on this secure foundation. Where this is impossible due to time constraints on the study, secondary data should be reviewed as soon as possible and applied to the development of a conceptual model of coastal behavior that should then inform the primary data collection methodology.

Table 3.3 outlines the basic attributes of a secondary database. Spatial data in the form of maps, charts, and remote sensed imagery should be made available in GIS format, allowing temporal and spatial comparisons.

REFERENCES

Appendini, C., P. Salles, E. Mendoza, J. Lopez, and A. Torres-Freyermuth. 2012. "Longshore Sediment Transport on the Northern Coast of the Yucatán Peninsula." *Journal of Coastal Research* 28 (6): 1404–17.

Bezaury, J., C. Santos, J. McCann, C. Islas, J. Carranza, P. Rubinoff, G. Townsend, D. Robadue, and L. Hale. 1998. "Participatory Coastal and Marine Management in Quintana Roo, Mexico." *Proceedings: International Tropical Marine Ecosystems Management Symposium (ITMEMS),* Townsville, Australia, November 23–26.

Blum, D., A. Carter, T. Zayac, and R. Goble. 2002. "Middle Holocene Sea Level and Evolution of the Gulf of Mexico Coast (USA)." *Journal of Coastal Research* SI 36: 65–80.

Castillo, S., P. Jean, and P. Moreno-Casasola. 1991. "Coastal Sand Dune Vegetation of Tabasco and Campeche, Mexico." *Journal of Vegetation Science* 2: 72–88.

Church, J. A., P. U. Clark, A. Cazenave, J. M. Gregory, S. Jevrejeva, A. Levermann, M. A. Merrifield, G. A. Milne, R. S. Nerem, P. D. Nunn, A. J. Payne, W. T. Pfeffer, D. Stammer, and A. S. Unnikrishnan. 2013. "Sea Level Change." In *Climate Change 2013: The Physical Science Basis. Contribution of Working Group I to the Fifth Assessment Report of the Intergovernmental Panel on Climate Change.* Cambridge, UK, and New York, NY: Cambridge University Press.

Conner, W., J. Day, M. Baumann, and J. Randall. 1989. "Influence of Hurricanes on Coastal Ecosystems along the Northern Gulf of Mexico." *Wetland Ecology and Management* 1: 45–56.

David, L., and B. Kjerfve. 1998. "Tides and Currents in a Two-Inlet Coastal Lagoon: Laguna de Terminos, Mexico." *Continental Shelf Research* 18: 1057–79.

Diez, J., M. Esteban, and R. Paz. 2008. "Cancún Barrier: Alternatives for Beach Restoration." Paper 199, Coastal and Port Engineering in Developing Countries (COPEDEC) VII, UEA, Dubai.

Diez, J., M. Esteban, and R. Paz. 2009. "Cancún-Nizuc Coastal Barrier." *Journal of Coastal Research* 25 (1): 57–68.

Emmanuel, K. 2005. "Increasing Destructiveness of Tropical Cyclones over the Past 30 Years (Letter)." *Nature* 436 (4): 686–88.

González-Leija, M., I. Mariño-Tapia, R. Silva, C. Enriquez, E. Mendoza, E. Escalante-Mancera, F. Ruiz-Renteria, and E. Uc-Sánchez. 2013. "Morphodynamic Evolution and Sediment Transport Processes of Cancún Beach." *Journal of Coastal Research* 29 (5): 1146–57.

Gutierrez-Estrada, M., A. Castro-Del Rio, and A. Galaviz-Solis. 1988. "Mexico". In *Artificial Structures and Shorelines*, edited by H. J. Walker, 669–78. Dordrecht, Netherlands: Kluwer Academic Publishers.

Harms, J., P. Choquette, and M. Brady. 1978. "Carbonate Sand Waves, Isla Mujeres, Yucatán. Geology and Hydrogeology of N E Yucatán." *New Orleans Geological Society* 60–84.

Kjerfve, B. 1994. *Coastal Oceanographic Characteristics, Cancún-Tulum Corridor, Quintana Roo.* Programa de Ecologia, Pesquerias y Oceanografia del Golfo de Mexico. Universidad Autonoma de Campeche: 1–35.

Loucks, R., and W. Ward. 2001. "Eolian Stratification and Beach to Dune Transition in a Holocene Carbonate Eolinite Complex, Cancún, Quintana Roo, Mexico." *Sedimentary Geology Special Publication* 71: 57–76.

Meyer-Arendt, K. 1991. "Tourism Development on the North Yucatán Coast." *GeoJournal* 23 (4): 327–36.

Nicholls, R. J., N. Marinova, J. A. Lowe, S. Brown, P. Vellinga, D. de Gusmão, J. Hinkel, and R. S. J. Tol. 2011. "Sea Level Rise and Its Possible Impacts Given A 'Beyond 4°C World' in the Twenty-First Century." *Philosophical Transactions of the Royal Society of London* Series A 369: 161–81.

Perry, E., G. Velazquez-Oliman, and R. A. Socki. 2003. "Hydrogeology of the Yucatán Peninsula." In *21st Symposium on Plant Biology*, edited by A. Pompa and S. Fedick, 115–38. Binghamton, NY: Haworth Press.

Phleger, F., and A. Ayala-Castanares. 1971. "Processes and History of Terminos Lagoon, Mexico." *American Association of Petroleum Geologists Bulletin* 55 (12): 2130–40.

Psuty, N. 1965. "Beach-Ridge Development in Tabasco, Mexico." *Annals of the Association of American Geographers* 55: 112–24.

Rivera-Arriaga, E., and G. Villalobos-Zapata. 2005. "The Coastal Zone of Campeche, Mexico: Opportunities for Implementing an Integrated Coastal Management Framework." *Journal of Coastal Research* 42: 184–90.

Thom, B. T. 1967 "Mangrove Ecology and Deltaic Geomorphology: Tabasco, Mexico." *Journal of Ecology* 55 (2): 301–43.

Vanegas, G., E. Serratos, and R. Casarin. 2013. *Peligros Naturales en el Estado de Campeche. Cuantificación y Protección Civil.* Campeche: Universidad Autónoma de Campeche, CENECAM-Gobierno del Estado de Campeche, CENAPRED.

Ward, W., and M. Brady. 1973. "High Energy Carbonates on the Inner Shelf, NE Yucatán Peninsula." *Transactions—Gulf Coast Association of Geological Societies* 23: 226–38.

Ward, W., A. Weidie, and W. Back. 1985. "Geology and Hydrogeology of the Yucatán and Quaternary Geology of the North-Eastern Yucatán Peninsula." *New Orleans Geological Society* i–v.

Webster, P., G. Holland, J. Curry, and H.-R. Chang. 2005. "Changes in Tropical Cyclone Number, Duration, and Intensity in a Warming Environment." *Science* 309 (5742): 1844–46.

4 Cost of Natural Disasters and Climate Change Implications

ELENA STRUKOVA GOLUB

INTRODUCTION

Like much of the Caribbean, the Yucatán Peninsula lies within the Atlantic Hurricane Belt. Because of its almost uniformly flat terrain, the peninsula is particularly vulnerable to the large storms coming from the east. Map 4.1 presents tracks of all hurricanes, tropical storms, and tropical depressions that hit Yucatán in 1970–2014.

A preliminary analysis was conducted on the data on floods, storms, and rains that are associated with the wet air masses that moved over the Atlantic and hit the Yucatán Peninsula. This analysis shows an increase in the frequency of extreme weather events, as well as growing damages per event. These trends could be largely attributed to an increase in land and water temperature in the region, which has been linked to climate change (Government of Yucatán 2012).

If global temperatures were to continue this upward trend, temperatures in the region would also continue to rise and would likely be associated with an increase in the frequency and severity of extreme weather events. Table 4.1 summarizes projections of future temperature change and other climate change indicators for the State of Yucatán.

FREQUENCY AND INTENSITY OF EXTREME WEATHER EVENTS IN THE YUCATÁN PENINSULA

Estimating climate change impacts is difficult, among other reasons, because of the high uncertainty in the dynamics that influence the intensity and magnitude of extreme weather events. One approach to deal with such uncertainty is to conduct a probabilistic analysis to cover a wide range of possible climate change scenarios. To this end, projections from the DICE 2009 model (Nordhaus 2010) were applied to compute an increase of global temperature from pre-industrial level up to 2050. While the probabilistic analysis helps to address some sources

MAP 4.1

Tracks of hurricanes, tropical storms, and tropical depressions that hit Yucatán, 1970–2014

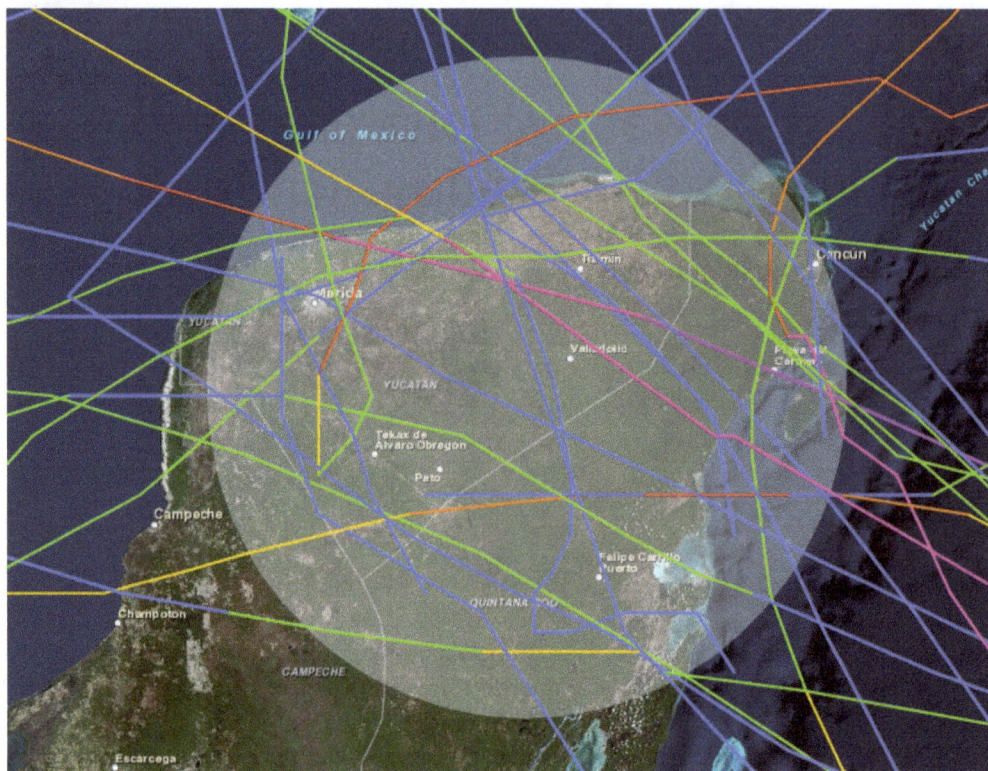

Source: NOAA 2016a.
Note: Green = tropical storm; Blue = tropical depression; Yellow = hurricane category 1 (sustained winds of 119–153 km/h); Orange = hurricane category 2 (sustained winds of 154–177 km/h); Red = hurricane category 3 (sustained winds of 178–208 km/h); Pink = hurricane category 4 (sustained winds of 209–251 km/h).

TABLE 4.1 Summary of projections of future temperature change and other projected indicators of climate change for Yucatán

INDICATOR	2020	2050	2080
Temperature increase in C°	0.5–0.8	0.5–1.8	0.6–2.8
Variation of annual precipitation (%)	(−14.9%)–1%	(−14.9%)–1%	(−14.9%)–1%
Number of extremely hot days/year	7–12	9–51	10–78
Number of extremely cold days/year	19–8	26–8	33–9
Annual reduction of extremely wet days	0–13	0–13	0–13
Annual increase of extremely dry days	(−4)–16	(−4)–16	(−4)–16

Source: Government of Yucatán 2012.

of uncertainty, their results are challenged by global emission scenarios and unknown parameters of the climatic system.

For this analysis, the "optimal CO_2 emission scenario" from the DICE 2009 model was used. Results of DICE 2009 are consistent with the range for temperature change that table 4.1 presents. Therefore, the analysis presented in this chapter was conducted using global temperature as a major exogenous parameter and presenting frequency and severity of extreme weather events as a function of global temperature increase.

Available data shows an increase in the frequency of extreme weather events in the Yucatán Peninsula after 1985 (figure 4.1). Improvements in the reporting system could explain such an increase, but it can also be attributed to climate change. Based on this historical data, future scenarios were projected by linking the frequency of extreme weather events with global temperature increases, which were developed using estimations of decadal temperature trends from NOAA (2016b) The analysis also estimated the relationship between extreme weather event frequency in Yucatán Peninsula and global temperature for the period 1970–2011 and 1990–2011. These two periods show a different quality in registration and reporting of extreme weather events in Mexico.

The analysis revealed a stronger relationship between the frequency of extreme weather events and temperature increase in Yucatán Peninsula. This relationship is about 35 percent stronger for the 1990–2011 period, compared with the 1970–2011 time frame.

The same methodology was used to analyze intensity of extreme weather events. The intensity of these events can be approximated by estimating the economic cost for each event, including its direct and indirect costs. In this analysis, only the costs of floods, rain and storm events were estimated for Yucatán Peninsula, because they are extreme natural meteorological events associated with climate change that result in significant loss of life and assets.

The deadliest natural disasters in Yucatán took place in 1990. Overall mortality trends have remained relatively constant for the last 40 years in Mexico, but mortality from extreme weather events has fallen slightly, to the credit of official efforts to improve preparedness to these events. However, despite these efforts, the number of people affected by extreme events has increased significantly over the last 20 years (figure 4.2).

FIGURE 4.1

Registered extreme weather events in the Yucatán Peninsula, number, and trends (linear and polynomial) over 40 years

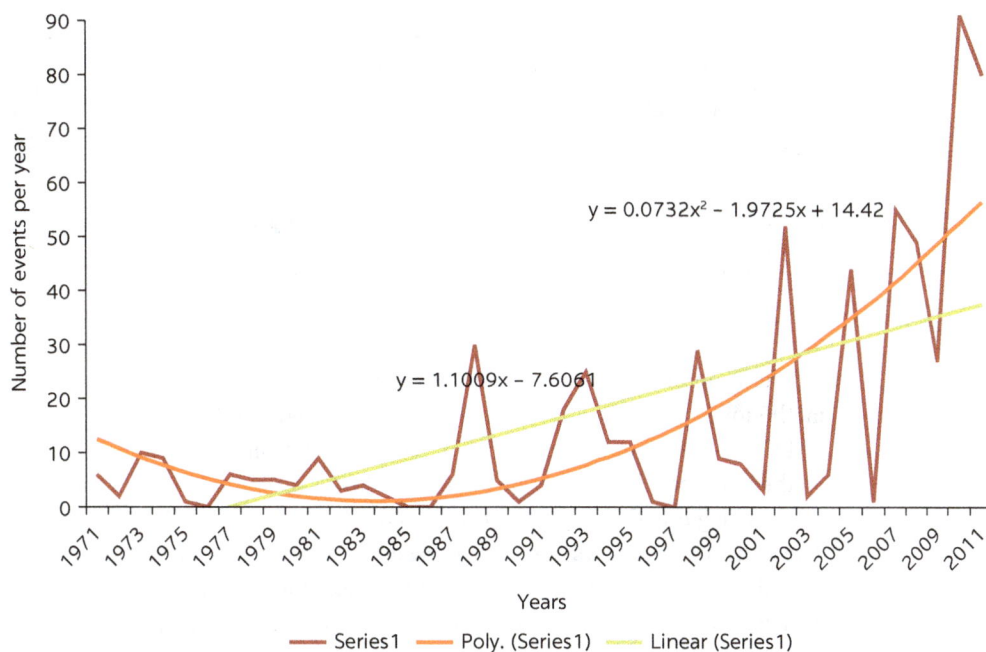

$$y = 0.0732x^2 - 1.9725x + 14.42$$

$$y = 1.1009x - 7.6061$$

Series1 — Poly. (Series1) — Linear (Series1)

Source: Golub 2015, based on United Nations Office for Disaster Risk Reduction (UNISDR) 2015b.

FIGURE 4.2

Dead, missing, and affected people in natural disasters in Yucatán

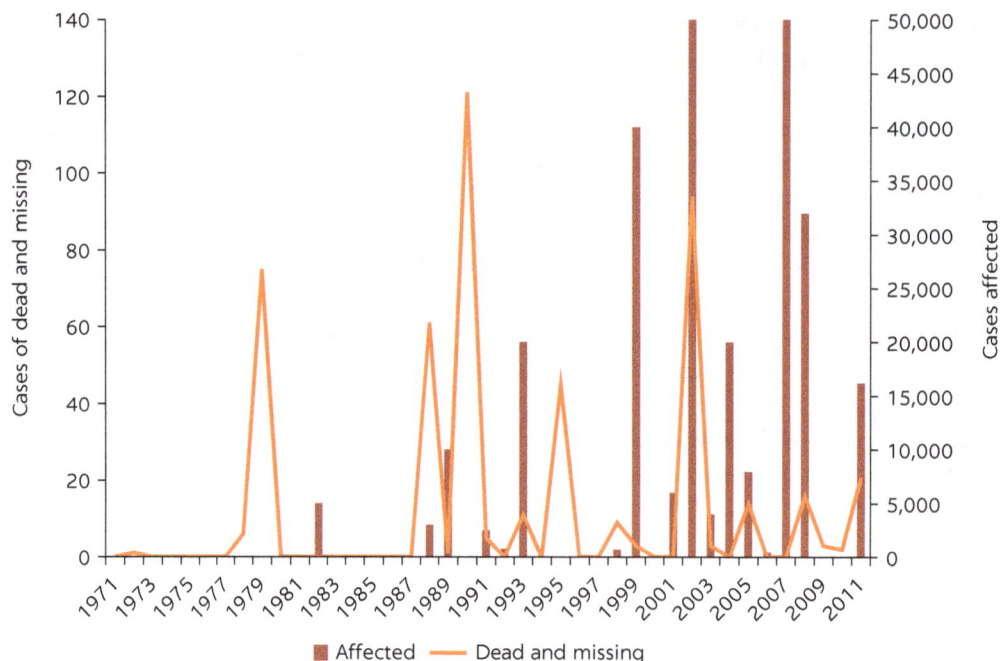

Source: Golub 2015, based on data from UNISDR (2015).

TABLE 4.2 Estimated annual direct cost of natural disasters (Mex$, million/unit)

LOSSES	COST PER CASE (MEX$)	PERCENT OF VALUE LOST (%)
People killed, missing	4,700,000	100
People affected	16,104	30
Houses destroyed	300,000	100
Houses affected	300,000	30
Schools affected	300,000	30
Medical centers affected	300,000	30
Total hectares of crops lost	6,739	100
Total livestock lost	2,138	100

Source: Golub 2015, based on information provided in PreventionWeb maintained by UNISDR (2015c).
Note: Estimated taking into account indirect cost as in UNISDR (2013).

The economic damage caused by each disaster was estimated using the methodology of value at risk from the report by UNISDR (2013) (table 4.2). In addition, the cost of mortality risk was estimated using a methodology based on the Value of a Statistical Life (VSL). The losses of affected people were estimated using one third of Mexico's gross domestic product (GDP) per capita. The value of homes was estimated based on Heston (2013), while those of schools and medical centers were approximated at the same value. Natural disasters also affect productivity of agricultural lands. Thus, the marginal profit per hectare was estimated using the values in Golub (2014), while the cost of one livestock unit lost was based on the data reported by UNISDR (2015a) and (Golub 2014).

The value at risk analysis relies on a description of the intensity and recurrence of natural hazards using a probability distribution function. Although historical data can often be used to project the occurrence of specific events in the future, this is not the case in the context of climate change, under which the intensity and frequency of extreme events is constantly changing. To address this challenge, the frequency of natural disasters was estimated based on reports available from UNISDR's (2015b) Disaster Information Management System.

After the natural hazards were characterized, the analysis established a damage function for a given hazard, taking into account the exposure and fragility of the population, ecosystems and economy. In this case, the application of past observations can be used to establish a baseline, but not necessarily as a future predictor because the exposure and sensitivity of population, ecosystems, and economy could change over time. For example, Mechler (2005) refers to an increase of population and economic growth with higher assets accumulation in Mexico as a factor that increases exposure to natural hazards. The analysis estimated the mean direct and indirect losses for the last 40-year period.

The analysis sought to assess the existence of significant effects based on a nonlinear response of intensity of extreme weather events with respect to global temperature change. None of these nonlinear linkages was identifiable because of information quality; hence, the increase of intensity of extreme weather events in Yucatán Peninsula was modeled as a linear function of global temperature increase.

During the reported period, there were 3 years (1988–90) with a very high cost per event. The largest was associated with the impact of hurricane Gilbert in 1988. Total losses for that event are several magnitudes higher than the average annual value. This kind of event cannot be analyzed based on available data and requires additional consideration. The analysis should consider the possibility that a similar or even higher-magnitude event may happen any time, albeit with a very low probability (available data suggest a return period of 50 years). The intensity observed in 1989 and 1990 is also rare, but the return period is about 20 years (figure 4.3).

The analysis estimated the structure of the cost of extreme weather events, based on the 6 years with the highest cost (figure 4.4). The total cost structure is estimated excluding the Gilbert hurricane year of 1988, because local costs that year were an order of magnitude higher than the average for the other years.

Infrequent major natural disasters with large impacts have a significantly different structure of impacts than similar low-impact but higher frequency events (figure 4.4). For the most devastating events, losses accrued by local businesses account for a major fraction of the total cost, while tourism and infrastructure losses also constitute a major component of local losses (Government of Yucatán 2012). Based on the analysis of historical data, the following section provides an outlook for economic losses associated with extreme weather events resulting from climate change.

FIGURE 4.3

Histogram of cost per extreme weather event, 1970–2011 in Yucatán Peninsula

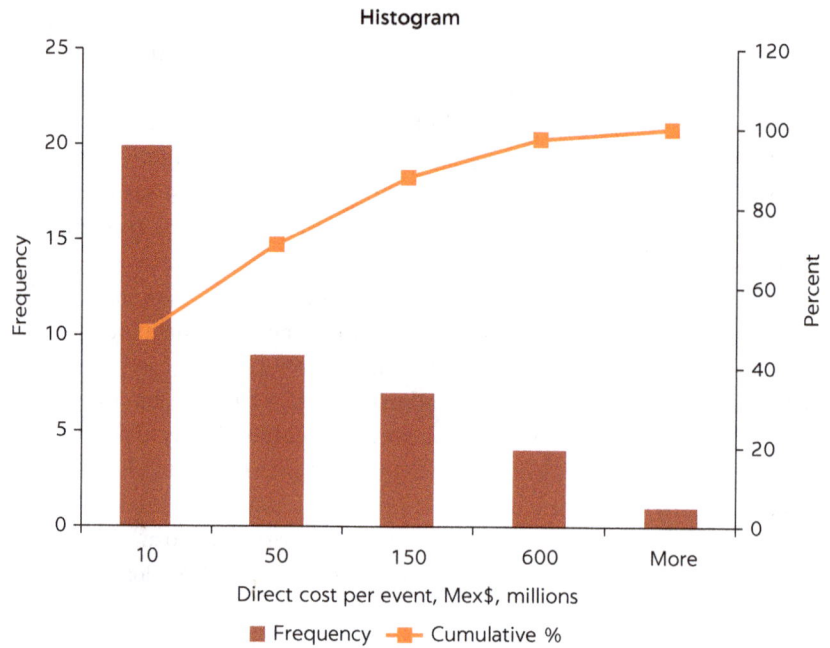

Source: Golub 2015.

FIGURE 4.4

Economic cost structure for extreme weather events in the Yucatán Peninsula

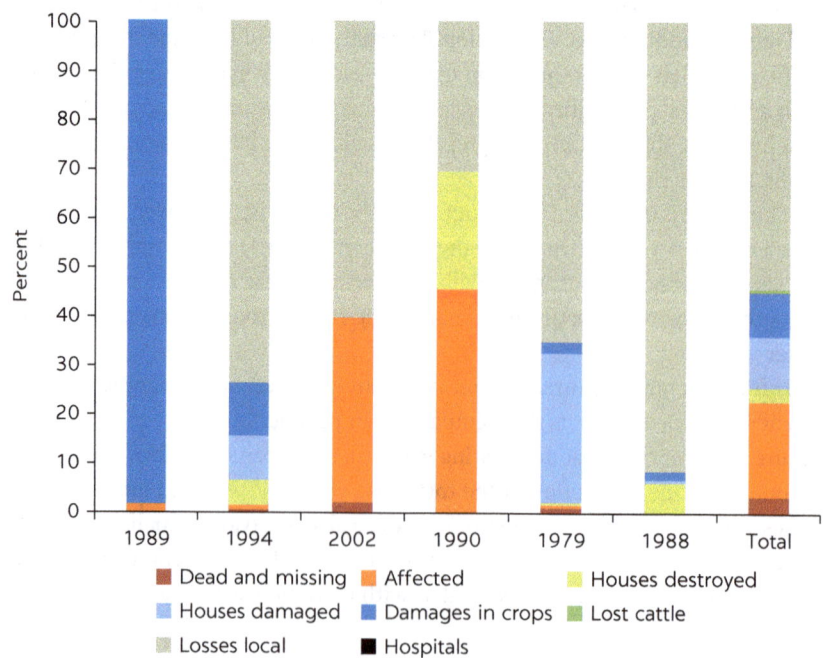

Source: Golub 2014.

ECONOMIC LOSSES ASSOCIATED WITH EXTREME WEATHER EVENTS AS RESULT OF CLIMATE CHANGE

The analysis applied a special climatic model to address uncertainties attributed to climate sensitivity and other major climatic system parameters. This model translates global GHG emissions into global temperature increase, based on the DICE 2009 model. Due to a high level of uncertainty of value of the economic losses, the analysis includes a Monte Carlo simulation to assess combined uncertainties and to compute the distribution for the output parameters (that is, annual economic cost of extreme weather events in Yucatán Peninsula in 2020–50).

Figure 4.5 presents the distribution of the economic cost function for the selected scenario. The results show that the most damaging event may happen with relatively low, but still significant, probability. The figure illustrates shifts in the annual expected economic cost associated with extreme weather events. This shift is attributed to a positive feedback between global temperature increases and growing frequency and intensity of extreme weather events. The probability density function of damage shifts right over time. Expected annual economic losses are relatively modest, in the order of Mex\$6–17 billion; however, there is a significant tail risk that reflects a combined uncertainty of global temperature increase, and intensity and frequency of individual events. However, a high-end tail risk is at least a magnitude below the reported losses for major events.

The characteristics of the distribution of the annual economic cost of extreme weather events for the Yucatán Peninsula are presented in table 4.3. These costs are estimated using a probabilistic model that links global temperature change and annual economic damage as described above.

If GDP were to grow 2–3 percent annually in the three states in the Yucatán Peninsula, the annual mean economic cost of extreme weather events (ordinary events) would be about 0.4 percent of GDP. This figure is about twice more than

FIGURE 4.5

Annual anticipated economic cost associated with extreme weather events in 2020, 2035, and 2060 (Mex\$, 10⁹)

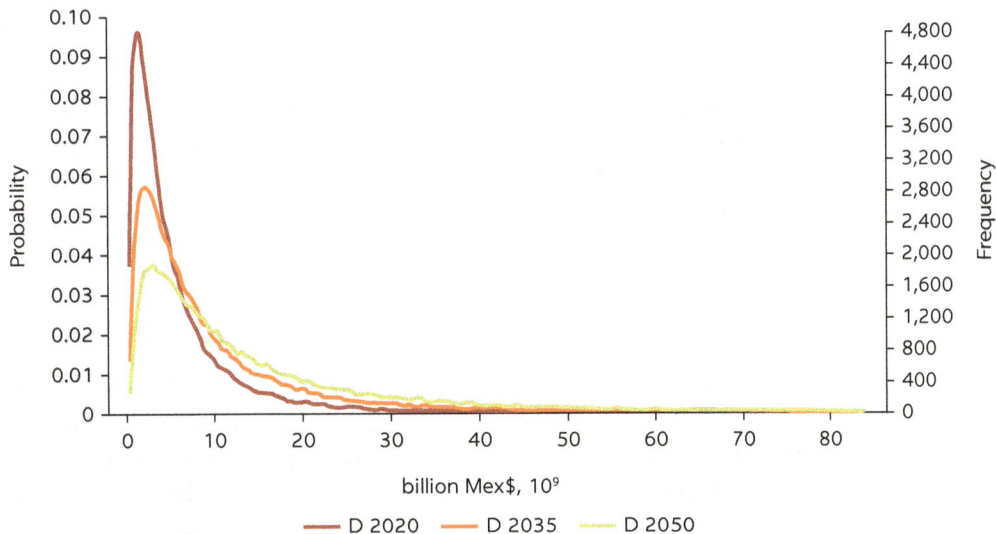

Source: Golub 2015.

TABLE 4.3 Economic losses associated with extreme weather events by year (Mex$, 10^9)

STATISTICS	2020	2025	2030	2035	2040	2045	2050
Mean	6.09	7.53	9.02	10.73	12.66	14.67	17.17
Median	3.69	4.46	5.34	6.33	7.33	8.58	9.80
Standard Deviation	7.84	10.34	12.35	14.41	17.61	20.13	24.39
Skewness	5.14	7.00	6.88	5.38	5.70	5.53	6.10
Kurtosis	57.02	121.46	110.90	62.51	68.46	61.50	81.34
Percentiles							
5%	0.67	0.79	0.94	1.08	1.22	1.41	1.58
10%	0.99	1.16	1.40	1.62	1.82	2.13	2.41
15%	1.29	1.51	1.79	2.08	2.39	2.80	3.15
20%	1.57	1.85	2.20	2.58	2.96	3.46	3.91
25%	1.85	2.21	2.63	3.08	3.55	4.15	4.71
30%	2.16	2.57	3.08	3.62	4.17	4.87	5.55
35%	2.49	2.97	3.57	4.20	4.86	5.66	6.44
40%	2.86	3.40	4.10	4.85	5.59	6.51	7.45
45%	3.26	3.90	4.69	5.54	6.42	7.49	8.55
50%	3.69	4.46	5.34	6.33	7.33	8.58	9.80
55%	4.20	5.07	6.08	7.24	8.37	9.79	11.23
60%	4.79	5.80	6.94	8.29	9.60	11.21	12.85
65%	5.47	6.61	7.96	9.48	11.04	12.88	14.76
70%	6.29	7.61	9.22	10.93	12.74	14.94	17.10
75%	7.31	8.95	10.77	12.72	14.90	17.41	20.13
80%	8.62	10.63	12.77	15.10	17.71	20.60	24.10
85%	10.45	12.96	15.60	18.43	21.73	25.13	29.71
90%	13.28	16.73	20.00	23.82	28.10	32.58	38.40
95%	19.38	24.16	28.57	34.80	41.03	47.51	55.76

Source: Golub 2015.
Note: Assuming DICE optimal CO_2 emission scenario and conservative assumptions regarding increase of frequency in response to temperature increase. DICE = dynamic integrated climate economy.

the annual cost of natural disasters for Mexico as a whole (Golub 2014). However, in the 95th percentile (when the damages would be highest) this cost could reach 1.4–1.5 percent of GDP in 2020 and 1.6–2.3 percent of GDP in 2050 (Government of Yucatán 2012).

SUMMARY

This chapter has provided an economic valuation of potential damages from meteorological events associated with climate change. The estimates presented in this chapter are based on economic valuation methods associated with probabilistic events. As noted in this chapter, the uncertainty in cost estimates remains significant and may differ considerably depending also on the geographical incidence and timing of the event. However, what emerges clearly from this analysis is a trend of ever-increasing cost impacts. Avoiding even a small portion of such costs through appropriate emergency preparedness, risk mitigation, or similar programs would be money well spent. Integrated coastal zone management (ICZM) efforts that reduce vulnerability to these significant hazards are an important adaptation mechanism. These efforts should consider both relatively infrequent, but catastrophic events, as well as events with less severe impacts, but that occur frequently.

This chapter also demonstrates that economic valuation can be helpful in communicating risks and in identifying priorities. In the overall ICZM context, such valuations can also be conducted to determine the economic impacts of other hazards (for example, water pollution, air pollution, and soil contamination), which may be hypothesized to be relevant in specific local circumstances. To date, the only such analysis to have been undertaken for the Yucatán Peninsula is that summarized in chapter 5 of this report. However, more-comprehensive analyses could be pursued as part of a broader priority-setting exercise to determine which issues have the most significant potential economic impacts.

REFERENCES

Gobierno de Yucatán. 2012. *Análisis de la vulnerabilidad actual y futura ante los efectos del cambio climático.* Programa Especial de Acción ante el Cambio Climático del Estado de Yucatán. Mérida: Gobierno del Estado de Yucatán. http://www.ccpy.gob.mx/agenda-yucatan /programa-estatal-estudios-peacc.php.

Heston, A. 2013. "Measuring the Real Size of the World Economy: The Framework, Methodology, and Results of the International Comparison Program—ICP." Washington, DC: World Bank.

Mechler, R. 2005. *Cost-Benefit Analysis of Natural Disaster Risk Management in Developing Countries. Manual.* Bonn: GTZ (German Agency for Technical Cooperation (Deutsche Gesellschaft für Technische Zusammenarbeit—GTZ; replaced by German Agency for International Cooperation—Deutsche Gesellschaft für Internationale Zusammenarbeit— GIZ).

NOAA (National Ocean and Atmospheric Administration). 2016a. "Historical Hurricane Tracks (Dataset)." http://coast.noaa.gov/hurricanes.

———. 2016b. "Climate at a Glance (dataset)." http://www.ncdc.noaa.gov/cag.

Nordhaus W. D. 2010. "RICE-2010 and DICE-2010 Models (as of August 25, 2010)." http://www .econ.yale.edu/~nordhaus/homepage/RICEmodels.htm.

UNISDR (United Nations Office for Disaster Risk Reduction). 2013. *Global Assessment Report on Disaster Risk Analysis. Annex 2. Loss Data and Extensive/Intensive Risk Analysis.* Geneva: UNISDR.

———. 2015a. *Global Assessment Report on Disaster Risk Reduction. Annex 2.* Geneva: UNISDR.

———. 2015b. "Disaster Information Management System (DESINVENTAR)." http://www .desinventar.net.

———. 2015c. "PreventionWeb." http://www.preventionweb.net.

5 The Cost of Environmental Degradation in the Yucatán Peninsula

BJORN LARSEN AND JOHN MAGNE SKJELVIK

INTRODUCTION

In the Yucatán Peninsula, as practically everywhere else, government agencies have limited resources to develop policies and support interventions that will contribute to sustainable development. Having a rigorous methodology to set priorities is therefore essential to ensure that scarce public resources target the environmental issues that cause the most severe social and economic impacts, and particularly those that affect primarily the poor and other vulnerable groups.

A methodologically rigorous approximation to identify environmental priorities is to quantify the impacts and economic costs of these issues.[1] As part of this analysis, economic valuation techniques were used to estimate the cost of environmental degradation impacts on human health, and thus on economic and social development and well-being.[2] To estimate these impacts, the first part of the analysis calculated the number of deaths and cases of illnesses caused by environmental problems with well-established health effects, particularly household (indoor) air pollution, outdoor air pollution, lead exposure, and inadequate water supply, sanitation, and hygiene (WSH). These calculations relied on available data at the state and national levels, as well as on an extensive literature review. Where possible and relevant, risks were estimated based on the specific characteristics of stakeholders, such as age group, or urban vs. rural settings. For example, because indoor air pollution occurs within home dwellings, its impacts for different households can be more easily evaluated. Other categories of environmental degradation—such as outdoor air pollution or exposure to lead—occur in areas where the differentiation of effects across different stakeholder groups cannot be measured using the available resources and data.

After estimating the health impacts of the environmental risks, the analysis quantified the economic losses that they represent. These losses come in many forms, including loss of income, productivity, and contributions to household activities due to premature mortality, illness, and neuropsychological impairments (IQ losses). Illness also involves cost of medical treatment. These costs were quantified in monetary terms by means of valuation techniques used in economics.

The cost of premature mortality was estimated by using a value of statistical life (VSL), which is based on individuals' willingness-to-pay (WTP) for a reduction in the risk of death. The VSL applied to the Yucatán Peninsula is Mex$5.9 million or US$461 thousand. This is somewhat over 50 times the Gross Regional Income (GRI) per capita in the peninsula in 2013. The cost of IQ losses is estimated based on the present value of the reduction in lifetime income.

The cost of illness was calculated using two commonly used valuation techniques. The cost-of-illness (COI) approach integrates the cost of medical treatment and the value of income and time lost to illness. The second approach equates cost of illness to individuals' WTP for avoiding an episode of illness. Studies in many countries have found that individuals' WTP to avoid an episode of an acute illness is generally much higher than the cost of treatment and value of income and time losses (Alberini and Krupnick 2000; Cropper and Oates 1992; Dickie and Gerking 2002; Wilson 2003).

In this report, the cost of a day of illness is estimated as 50 percent of the average labor income in the Yucatán Peninsula. This figure is also applied to individuals without income, because illness prevents most of these individuals from undertaking household work and other activities with a social value. In addition to monetary values, estimates also reflect the effect of environmental degradation on Disability-adjusted life years (DALYs), an internationally accepted measure of years of healthy life lost due to diseases caused by environment degradation or other causes.

HEALTH AND ECONOMIC EFFECTS OF ENVIRONMENTAL DEGRADATION

Using conservative assumptions, this report estimates that 1,073–1,100 people died in the Yucatán Peninsula in 2013 from environmental health risks. Around 80 percent of the Yucatán deaths are from household and outdoor air pollution, while adult lead (Pb) exposure and inadequate water supply, sanitation, and hygiene caused 13 percent and 7 percent of total deaths, respectively. In addition to these premature deaths, environmental health risks also caused millions of cases of illness and impaired intelligence among children (table 5.1).

TABLE 5.1 **Annual deaths and days of illness from environmental risk factors in the Yucatán Peninsula, 2013**

	DEATHS			DAYS OF ILLNESS (000)		
	LOW	MID	HIGH	LOW	MID	HIGH
Lead (Pb) exposure— adults	138	138	138	337	505	674
Household air pollution	524	538	551	2,065	3,204	4,343
Outdoor air pollution	332	332	332	812	1,219	1,625
Water, sanitation, hygiene	79	79	79	3,748	4,287	4,909
Total	**1,073**	**1,087**	**1,100**	**7,049**	**9,357**	**11,747**

Source: Larsen and Skjelvik 2015.
Note: Additional impacts of lead exposure are 87–197 thousand lost IQ points per year among children under five years of age.

TABLE 5.2 Estimated annual cost of environmental health effects in the Yucatán Peninsula, 2013

	COST (MEX$, MILLIONS)			COST (PERCENT OF GRI)		
	LOW	MID	HIGH	LOW (%)	MID (%)	HIGH (%)
Lead (Pb) exposure	4,332	6,529	8,726	0.88	1.33	1.77
Household air pollution	3,297	3,498	3,688	0.67	0.71	0.75
Outdoor air pollution	2,120	2,200	2,281	0.43	0.45	0.46
Water, sanitation, hygiene	1,190	1,294	1,415	0.24	0.26	0.29
Total	**10,939**	**13,521**	**16,110**	**2.22**	**2.75**	**3.27**

Source: Larsen and Skjelvik 2015.

The health effects from the environmental risk factors can be monetized by using standard valuation techniques in order to provide an economic perspective of the magnitude of these effects. The annual cost of the environmental health effects is estimated in the range of Mex$10,900–16,100 million in 2013, with a midpoint estimate of Mex$13,500 million. This cost is equivalent to 2.2–3.3 percent of the Yucatán Peninsula's estimated GRI in 2013, with a midpoint estimate of 2.75 percent (table 5.2).

About 48 percent of the cost is from lead (Pb) exposure, of which the vast majority is from impaired intelligence in children. Approximately 26 percent of the cost is from household air pollution, 16 percent is from outdoor air pollution, and 10 percent of the cost is from inadequate water, sanitation and hygiene. This last cost, however, does not include substantial non-health costs such as cost of bottled water purchased associated with public perceptions of health risk associated with piped water and water from wells.

LEAD (PB) EXPOSURE

As these figures indicate, lead (Pb) exposure is the environmental health risk with the highest cost. Lead in the human body can originate from exposure to lead in air, drinking water, food, dust, soil, paint, cosmetics, utensils, several herbal medicines, children's toys, ornaments and jewelry, and other materials and articles containing lead. Identified sources of lead in Mexico include glazed ceramics used for cooking and food storage, metal smelters, and mining waste (Acosta-Saavedra et al. 2011; Farias et al. 2014; Villalobos et al. 2009).

Studies in Mexico have found large declines in BLLs in the general population from the 1980s. Much of this decline is attributed to the phaseout of leaded gasoline. A review of 83 studies with 150 measurement samples of over 50,000 participants concluded that Blood Lead Levels (BLLs) in Mexican children declined from nearly 20 µg/dL prior to 1980 to around 5 µg/dL in the mid-2000s (Caravanos et al. 2014).

Based on the available data, it is estimated that the current average BBL in children under five years of age in Mexico City may be around 2.5–3.0 µg/dL, reflecting a likely continued decline in BLLs since the time of the last studies. BLLs in other urban areas of Mexico seem to be somewhat higher, around 3.5 µg/dL (Farias et al. 2014; Trejo-Acevedo et al. 2009). BLLs among rural children under five years of age are expected to be substantially higher than those of

FIGURE 5.1

Estimated blood-lead-level distribution in children under five in the Yucatán Peninsula, 2013

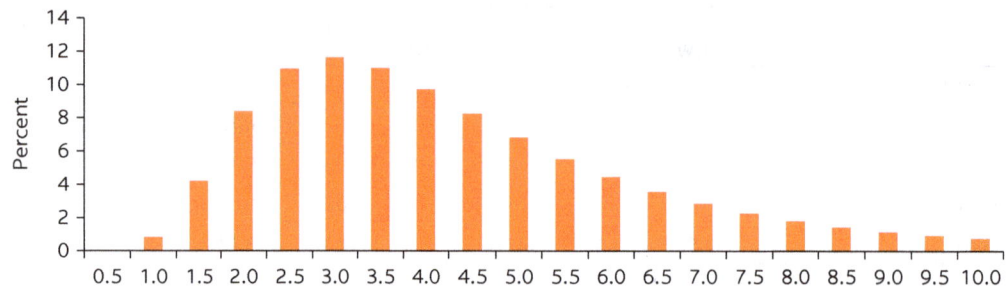

Source: Larsen and Skjelvik 2015.
Note: Mean urban and rural BLL of 3.5 and 5.5 µg/dL, respectively, with standard deviation (SD) of 1.70.

FIGURE 5.2

Estimated blood-lead-level distribution in adults 25+ years in the Yucatán Peninsula, 2013

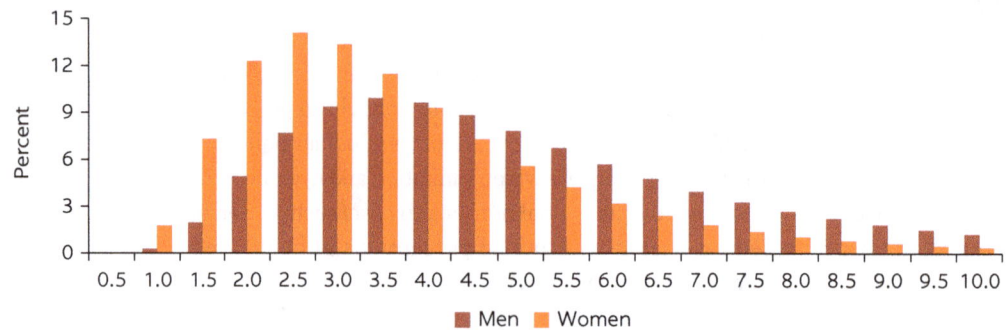

Source: Larsen and Skjelvik 2015.
Note: Men: Mean BLL = 4.35 µg/dL with standard deviation (SD) = 1.70. Women: Mean BLL = 3.05 µg/dL with SD = 1.7.

children in urban areas. One source of higher BLLs is the high prevalence of use of lead-glazed pottery for cooking and food storage, which was identified as a significant factor of high BLLs in Morelos by Farias et al. (2014). Caravanos et al (2014) found that rural BLLs were about 50–60 percent higher than urban BLL. Based on this information, an average BLL of 3.7 µg/dL among children under five years of age is estimated for the Yucatán Peninsula.

Very few recent studies of adult BLLs in Mexico were identified during the preparation of this report. In light of the BLLs among children, the current average BLL in adults of over 25 years of age in the Yucatán Peninsula may also be around 3.7 µg/dL. This would suggest a mean BLL of 4.35 µg/dL among males and 3.05 µg/dL among females, if the gender difference is similar to that observed in the United States.[3] Based on the above, it is estimated that 87 percent of children under five years of age, 79 percent of adult females, and 93 percent of male adults have a BLL of ≥ 2 µg/dL (figures 5.1 and 5.2).

A well-established effect of lead exposure is neuropsychological impairment in children, measured as IQ losses.[4] The effect is found to occur even at very low BLLs (Jusko et al. 2008; Lanphear et al. 2005; Surkan et al. 2007). In fact, no BLL

TABLE 5.3 **Estimated population blood lead levels by age group in the Yucatán Peninsula, 2013**

AGE (YEARS)	MEAN BLL (µg/dL) BY AGE GROUP	
	MALES	FEMALES
25–29	4.01	2.81
30–34	3.95	2.77
35–39	4.09	2.86
40–44	4.23	2.96
45–49	4.37	3.06
50–54	4.51	3.16
55–59	4.65	3.26
60–64	4.79	3.35
65–69	4.93	3.45
70–74	5.07	3.55
75–79	5.21	3.65
80+	5.35	3.75

Source: Larsen and Skjelvik 2015.

TABLE 5.4 **Estimated annual cardiovascular deaths from lead exposure by age group in the Yucatán Peninsula, 2013**

	25–39 YEARS	40–54 YEARS	55–69 YEARS	70+ YEARS	TOTAL
Ischemic heart disease	2	8	19	45	74
Cerebrovascular disease	1	5	11	26	43
Other vascular causes	1	3	5	12	21
Total	4	16	35	83	138

Source: Larsen and Skjelvik 2015.

threshold below which there are no impacts on children's IQ has been identified in the international research literature. Thus, this analysis estimates a total annual loss of 87–197 thousand IQ points among children under five years of age in the Yucatán Peninsula, with a midpoint estimate of 142 thousand.[5]

The main health effect of lead exposure among adults is the effect on systolic blood pressure (SBP) and consequent risk of cardiovascular disease (Lim et al. 2012). Estimating the cardiovascular disease burden from lead exposure requires calculating BLLs by age groups because the risk associated with a change in SBP varies by age (table 5.3).

A BLL lower threshold value of 2.0 µg/dL is applied in this report to estimate the cardiovascular disease burden from lead exposure. Based on this threshold, an estimated 138 deaths from lead exposure occurred in the Yucatán Peninsula in 2013 (table 5.4). About 40 percent of these deaths were among the population younger than 70 years. In addition, an estimated 185 disability years or 67 thousand disability days were lost from nonfatal cardiovascular disease. This corresponds to 337–674 thousand days of illness.[6]

HOUSEHOLD AIR POLLUTION

Household air pollution is the environmental challenge with the second highest economic costs. The severity of household air pollution is associated with the use of solid biomass fuels for cooking, as was done by 28 percent of Yucatán Peninsula's population in 2000. The highest prevalence was in the State of Yucatán (41 percent), followed by Campeche (35 percent). Only 2 percent of the population used solid fuels in Quintana Roo (Perez-Maldonado et al. 2011). This practice declined to 19 percent of the population in 2010, compared to 14.5 percent nationally.[7] By 2013 about 17 percent of the peninsula's population (around 190 thousand households), of which 70 percent reside in the State of Yucatán, would have used solid fuels if the trend from 2000 to 2010 continued.

Combustion of solid fuels generates several health damaging pollutants, including fine particulate matter (PM2.5), which causes several respiratory diseases. Measurement studies in Mexico and three other countries in Latin America have found 24–48 hours average PM2.5 concentrations in the kitchen area of about 130–1,020 µg/m³ among households that used wood for cooking over open fire or unimproved stoves. Some of the studies also measured 24–48 hours personal PM2.5 exposure, which averaged 120–264 µg/m³.

Based on available data, table 5.5 presents the estimated exposures to PM2.5 in households using solid fuels for cooking in the Yucatán Peninsula. In the absence of more-detailed exposure studies, a distribution from 75 to 250 µg/m³ is applied, with average personal exposures in the range of 144–173 µg/m³.[8] The distribution reflects an assumption that 15–25 percent of households using biomass cook with an improved chimney stove, and thus have estimated personal exposures in the range of 75–100 µg/m³.

The most substantial health effects of PM2.5 in the household environment are cardiovascular disease, chronic obstructive pulmonary disease (COPD), lung cancer among adults, and acute lower respiratory infections (ALRI) among young children (Lim et al. 2012). Table 5.6 presents the estimated relative risks of these disease outcomes from exposure to PM2.5 in the

TABLE 5.5 Estimated population exposure to PM2.5 in households using solid fuels in the Yucatán Peninsula, 2013

PM2.5 (µg/m³)	EXPOSURE DISTRIBUTION (PERCENT OF POPULATION)		
	LOW	CENTRAL	HIGH
75	2.1	1.7	1.3
100	2.1	1.7	1.3
125	3.2	2.7	2.4
150	3.2	2.7	2.4
175	3.2	2.7	2.4
200	3.2	2.7	2.4
225	0.0	2.7	2.4
250	0.0	0.0	2.4
Population using solid fuels	16.8	16.8	16.8
Population weighted PM2.5 (µg/m³)	144	158	173

Source: Larsen and Skjelvik 2015.

TABLE 5.6 **Relative risk of health effects associated with PM2.5 exposure**

PM2.5 (µg/m³)	ISCHEMIC HEART DISEASE	CEREBROVASCULAR DISEASE	COPD	LUNG CANCER	ALRI
0–7.3	1.0	1.0	1.0	1.0	1.0
75	1.4	1.7	1.3	1.4	1.8
250	1.6	2.2	1.8	2.0	2.7

Source: Larsen and Skjelvik 2015.
Note: ALRI = acute lower respiratory infections; COPD = chronic obstructive pulmonary disease.

TABLE 5.7 **Estimated annual deaths by cause and age in the Yucatán Peninsula from PM2.5 household air pollution, 2013**

HEALTH OUTCOME	< 5	25–39	40–54	55–69	70+	TOTAL
Ischemic heart disease	n.a.	12	37	65	108	222
Cerebrovascular disease	n.a.	7	28	50	105	190
COPD	n.a.	0	2	10	57	69
Lung cancer	n.a.	1	3	10	16	30
ALRI	27	n.a.	n.a.	n.a.	n.a.	27
Total	27	20	70	135	286	538

Source: Larsen and Skjelvik 2015.
Note: ALRI = acute lower respiratory infections; COPD = chronic obstructive pulmonary disease; n.a. = not applicable.

household environment. These risks are gender and age-weighted population averages.[9] An annual PM2.5 threshold of 7.3 µg/m³ is applied in this report, below which it is assumed that there are no health effects (Lim et al. 2012).

This report estimates that 524–551 people, with a central estimate of 538 persons, died from household PM2.5 air pollution in the Yucatán Peninsula in 2013 (table 5.7). Over 46 percent of the deaths were individuals younger than 70 years of age. Deaths caused by household air pollution represent 10 percent of total deaths in the Peninsula from these diseases. In addition, an estimated 1,131–1,190 disability years, or 413–434 thousand disability days were lost from nonfatal events of disease, which corresponds to 2.1–4.3 million days of illness.[10]

OUTDOOR AIR POLLUTION

Particulate matter (PM) and especially PM2.5 is the outdoor air pollutant that globally is associated with the largest health effects. Ambient PM2.5 air quality measurements in the Yucatán Peninsula are scarce. INECC's report on air quality in Mexico provides PM2.5 data only for the city of Merida, where annual average concentrations were 11 µg/m³ in 2013 (INECC 2014).

Recent nationwide and global estimates of PM2.5 concentrations using a combination of satellite-based measurements, chemical transport models, and, when available, ground level measurements represent an alternative to the single use of ground level measurements to estimate the health effects of PM2.5. Based on such data, Brauer et al. (2012) report that PM2.5 concentration levels in most Yucatán Peninsula locations are in the range of 5–10 µg/m³.

TABLE 5.8 Estimates of annual outdoor PM2.5 concentrations in the Yucatán Peninsula, 2013

PM2.5 (μg/m³)	MERIDA METROPOLITAN AREA	OTHER CITIES WITH POPULATION ≥ 100 THOUSAND (METROPOLITAN AREAS)	URBAN AREAS WITH POPULATION < 100 THOUSAND	RURAL AREAS	YUCATÁN PENINSULA
0–6	11.0%	15.0%	19.0%	35.0%	17.2%
6–9	15.0%	20.0%	25.0%	35.0%	21.7%
9–12	30.0%	35.0%	40.0%	25.0%	34.2%
12–15	30.0%	20.0%	10.0%	5.0%	18.0%
15–18	14.0%	10.0%	6.0%	0.0%	8.8%
Total	100%	100%	100%	100%	100%
Population (000), 2013[a]	1,050	1,560	1,260	430	4,300
Population-weighted PM2.5 (μg/m³)	11.0	10.0	9.0	7.0	9.6

Source: Larsen and Skjelvik 2015.
a. Estimate for 2013 based on Population Census 2010.

FIGURE 5.3

Relative risk of health effects associated with PM2.5 exposure at Yucatán Peninsula

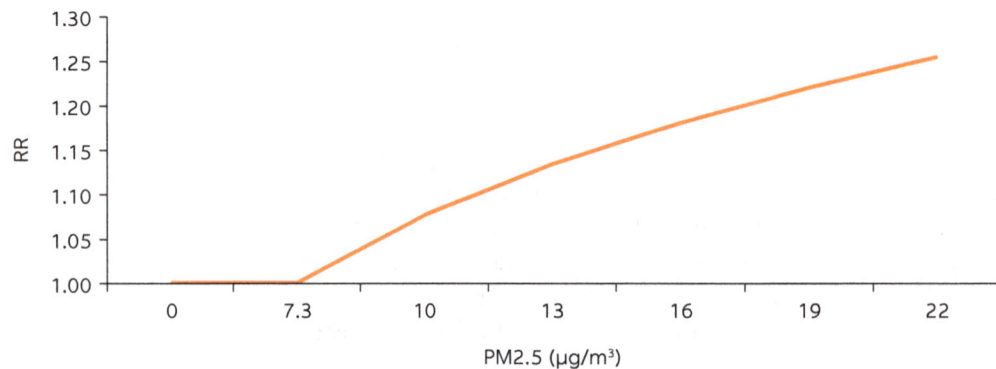

Source: Larsen and Skjelvik 2015.

Such spatially detailed estimates of PM2.5 enable an estimation of health effects in all urban and rural areas of the peninsula. However, these data and modeling may tend to underestimate concentrations in many cities; consequently, these data and modeling should be applied with caution (van Donkelaar et al. 2015).

In the absence of comprehensive ground-level monitoring of PM2.5 from the Yucatán Peninsula, estimates presented in Brauer et al. (2012) and ground-level monitoring from the city of Merida are here combined to provide estimates of annual PM2.5 concentrations throughout the peninsula for 2013. As PM2.5 concentrations vary within each city and urban area, and across rural areas, a population exposure distribution is derived as presented in table 5.8.

The most substantial health effects of PM2.5 are cardiovascular disease, COPD, lung cancer among adults, and ALRI among young children (Lim et al. 2012; Mehta et al. 2013; Pope et al. 2009, 2011). Figure 5.3 presents the estimated relative risks of these disease outcomes in relation to PM2.5 exposure. The risks are age-weighted population averages.

TABLE 5.9 **Estimated annual deaths across the Yucatán Peninsula from PM2.5 outdoor air pollution, 2013**

	ANNUAL DEATHS	SHARE (%)
Merida Metropolitan Area	98	29
Other cities with population ≥ 100 thousand	142	43
Urban areas with population < 100 thousand	78	23
Rural areas	14	4
Total	332	100

Source: Larsen and Skjelvik 2015.

TABLE 5.10 **Estimated annual deaths by cause and age in the Yucatán Peninsula from PM2.5 outdoor air pollution, 2013**

HEALTH OUTCOME	< 5 YRS	25–39 YRS	40–54 YRS	55–69 YRS	70+ YRS	TOTAL
Ischemic heart disease	n.a.	10	37	64	98	209
Cerebrovascular disease	n.a.	5	10	18	44	76
COPD	n.a.	1	1	4	25	31
Lung cancer	n.a.	0	1	4	7	13
ALRI	3	n.a.	n.a.	n.a.	n.a.	3
Total	3	16	49	90	174	332

Source: Larsen and Skjelvik 2015.
Note: ALRI = acute lower respiratory infections; COPD = chronic obstructive pulmonary disease; n.a. = not applicable.

This report applies an annual PM2.5 threshold of 7.3 μg/m³, below which it is assumed that there are no health effects. Based on the PM2.5 concentrations and exposure distributions in table 5.8, about 70 percent of the population at Yucatán Peninsula is exposed to PM2.5 levels associated with health effects.

Based on these estimates, 332 people died from outdoor PM2.5 air pollution in the Yucatán Peninsula in 2013. About 72 percent of these deaths were in the Merida Metropolitan Area and five other metropolitan areas with populations greater than 100 thousand (table 5.9). The deaths caused by outdoor air pollution represent around 6.5 percent of total deaths in the Yucatán Peninsula from these causes. Over 47 percent of the deaths from PM2.5 were individuals younger than 70 years of age. In addition, an estimated 445 disability years or 162 thousand disability days were lost from non-fatal events of disease. This corresponds to 0.8–1.6 million days of illness.[11]

INADEQUATE WATER SUPPLY, SANITATION, AND HYGIENE

According to the 2010 Population Census, nearly 92 percent of households in Mexico had piped water supply to their dwelling or yard. In the Yucatán Peninsula, this was higher, at about 94 percent of households.

The Joint Monitoring Programme for Water Supply and Sanitation (JMP) by WHO/UNICEF estimates that 85 percent of the Mexican population had access

TABLE 5.11 **Percent of households with water and sanitation services, 2010**

Percent

	CAMPECHE	QUINTANA ROO	YUCATÁN	PENINSULA
Piped water supply	90	92	97	94
Piped water on premises from public networks	84	88	93	90
Toilet facility	91	93	86	90
Piped drainage to sewer system or septic tank	85	91	79	84

Source: Mexico Population Census 2010.

TABLE 5.12 **Estimated deaths from inadequate water, sanitation, and hygiene by age group at the Yucatán Peninsula, 2013**

HEALTH OUTCOME	< 5	5–24	25–39	40–54	55–69	70+	TOTAL
Diarrheal diseases	24	7	4	5	8	27	75
Infectious diseases from child underweight	4	n.a.	n.a.	n.a.	n.a.	n.a.	4
Total	28	7	4	5	8	27	79

Source: Larsen and Skjelvik 2015.
Note: n.a. = not applicable.

to an improved and non-shared sanitation facility in 2011. An estimated 11 percent of the population shared a facility. According to the Population Census 2010, about 90 percent of the population had flush or pour-flush toilets connected to a piped sewer system or septic tank. According to the same Census about 90 percent of households in the Yucatán Peninsula had sanitation services in 2010 and 84 percent of the households have piped drainage to sewer system or septic tank (table 5.11).

In addition to good quality drinking water and sanitation, good hygiene practices are essential for infectious disease prevention. In particular, handwashing with soap at critical times has been found to substantially reduce diarrheal illness (Curtis and Cairncross 2003; Fewtrell et al. 2005; Ejemot et al. 2008; Waddington et al. 2009; Cairncross et al. 2010; Freeman et al. 2014). However, limited information is available on household and community hygiene practices and conditions in the Yucatán Peninsula, preventing this report from providing an assessment.

Inadequate WSH causes diarrhea and other infectious diseases. Poor sanitation and hygiene increases the risk of parasite infestation, while poor handwashing practices are a major contributor to diarrhea and respiratory infections in children (Rabie and Curtis 2006). Repeated diarrheal infections in early childhood contribute to poor nutritional status (for example, underweight), as evidenced by research studies in communities with a wide range of diarrheal infection rates in a diverse group of countries (World Bank 2008).

The health effects of inadequate WSH in the Yucatán Peninsula include diarrheal mortality and morbidity in children and adults, and child mortality from poor nutritional status caused by inadequate WSH. In particular, inadequate WSH caused 79 deaths in the peninsula in 2013 (table 5.12). This represents 46 percent of all deaths from diarrheal diseases including typhoid.[12]

About 35 percent of these deaths were among children under five years of age, and 34 percent were among the population older than 70 years. In addition, inadequate WSH caused an estimated 1.25–1.65 million cases of diarrheal disease, or 3.75–4.90 million days of illness.

SUMMARY

This chapter has identified and ranked the environmental risks that cause the most severe health and economic impacts in the Yucatán Peninsula. In particular, it summarized the result of an analysis that estimated that between 1,073 and 1,100 people died in the Yucatán Peninsula in 2013 from environmental health risks. In terms of mortality impacts in the peninsula, household air pollution is the most severe problem, followed by outdoor air pollution; these two types of air pollution are responsible for around 80 percent of deaths associated with an environmental health risk. Adult lead (Pb) exposure and inadequate water, sanitation and hygiene caused 13 percent and 7 percent of total deaths, respectively.

From an economic standpoint, the annual cost of the environmental health effects is estimated in the range of Mex$10,900–16,100 million in 2013, with a midpoint estimate of Mex$13,500 million. This cost is equivalent to 2.2–3.3 percent of Yucatán Peninsula's estimated GRI in 2013, with a midpoint estimate of 2.75 percent. Lead exposure is responsible for 48 percent of this cost, mostly because it results in impaired intelligence in children and a consequent reduction in lifetime earnings. About 26 percent of the cost is from household air pollution, 16 percent is from outdoor air pollution, and 10 percent of the cost is from inadequate water, sanitation and hygiene.

Thus, the analysis indicates that levels of exposure to environmental health risks in the Yucatán Peninsula are significant and result in a major loss of welfare, economic opportunities, and quality of life, particularly for lower income groups, such as households that still use biomass fuels. To address these challenges, the state governments of the Yucatán Peninsula could consider filling additional knowledge gaps and assessing interventions targeting environmental priority problems.

Although BLLs have been decreasing over time, efforts should be made to identify and control lead exposure in *hotspots*. In addition, in light of recent evidence of the severity of impacts of lead in children, measurement studies should be undertaken to confirm BLLs among children, map geographic pockets of high BLLs, and identify and control sources of lead exposure.

Given the significant health effects and high cost of household use of solid fuels for cooking, increased emphasis should be placed on improved cooking stoves, ventilation, and switching of fuel to LPG. When tackling both household and outdoor air pollution, governmental efforts should prioritize mitigating emissions and reducing concentration of PM2.5, which is the air pollutant with the largest health effects.

Finally, improvements should be continued in the water and sanitation sector, with emphasis on bridging the sanitation gap, ensuring good quality drinking water, and continuing efforts to improve handwashing practices and other hygiene dimensions.

Although the three state governments from the Yucatán Peninsula have begun to address shared challenges jointly, notably in the case of climate change, there is currently no priority setting mechanism in the region and the scarce available resources are not used to address the categories of environmental degradation that are causing the most significant effects. This study provides an urgently needed framework to align resources and efforts to achieve better environmental conditions. The methodologies and approach adopted by this analytical work can be replicated in the future to evaluate progress in reducing environmental conditions, identifying policy and intervention improvements, and determining the most efficient use of scarce resources. In doing so, it will be crucial to continuously incorporate new scientific findings, evolving methodologies, and broader stakeholder perspectives.

NOTES

1. The economic cost of environmental degradation is often valued by estimating the value of environmental externalities, or the cost borne by society even if market prices do not reflect the costs. An example is urban air pollution: Urban residents may suffer from pollution, but the pollution emitters are not charged for their pollution and are not required to compensate those who get sick.
2. The annex to Larsen and Skjelvik (2015) provides a description of all the methodologies used to quantify environmental priority problems.
3. Health effects among the adult population are estimated for individuals 25+ years of age in this report, as in the Global Burden of Disease 2010 study (Lim et al. 2012).
4. Intelligence quotient (IQ) is a score on standardized tests designed to assess intelligence.
5. Annual loss of IQ points is calculated as Δ IQ/5 by assuming that the children's IQ points are lost in the first five years of life.
6. This reflects a disability weight of 0.1–0.2. Several cardiovascular diseases are categorized in this range in the GBD 2010 Study.
7. Microdata from the Mexico Population and Housing Census 2010.
8. Personal exposures of 338 $\mu g/m^3$ among women, 285 $\mu g/m^3$ among children, and 205 $\mu g/m^3$ among men in households using solid fuels from studies in India formed the basis for the recent Global Burden of Disease (GBD) 2010 study (Smith et al. 2014). The exposure levels applied to the Yucatán Peninsula are substantially lower, based on the reviewed monitoring studies in several Latin American countries.
9. Note that the relative risk of ischemic heart disease and cerebrovascular disease changes little from 100 $\mu g/m^3$ to 400 $\mu g/m^3$ of PM2.5 concentrations. Since these two disease outcomes account for 70% of health effects from household air pollution, total estimated health effects are relatively insensitive to the population exposure distribution presented previously.
10. This reflects a disability weight of 0.1–0.2. Several cardiovascular diseases and moderate COPD are categorized in this range in the GBD 2010 Study.
11. This reflects a disability weight of 0.1–0.2. Several cardiovascular diseases and moderate COPD are categorized in this range in the GBD 2010 study.
12. Prüss-Ustün et al. (2014) attributes 46% of diarrheal disease to inadequate water, sanitation, and hygiene in Latin America. Globally, the attributable fraction is 58% among low- and middle-income countries. Infectious disease deaths from underweight among children under five years of age caused by diarrheal disease are very low, given that the prevalence of moderate and severe underweight in Mexico totals around 3%.

REFERENCES

Acosta-Saavedra, L. C., M. E. Moreno, T. Rodríguez-Kessler, A. Luna, R. Gomez, D. Arias-Salvatierra, and E. S. Calderon-Aranda. 2011. "Environmental Exposure to Lead and Mercury in Mexican Children: A Real Health Problem." *Toxicology Mechanisms and Methods* 21 (9): 656–66.

Alberini, A., and A. Krupnick. 2000. "Cost-of-Illness and Willingness-to-Pay Estimates of the Benefits of Improved Air Quality: Evidence from Taiwan." *Land Economics* 76: 37–53.

Brauer, M., M. Amann, R. T. Burnett, A. Cohen, F. Dentener, M. Ezzati, S. B. Henderson, M. Krzyzanowski, R. V. Martin, R. Van Dingenen, A. van Donkelaar, and G. D. Thurston. 2012. "Exposure Assessment for Estimation of the Global Burden of Disease Attributable to Outdoor Air Pollution." *Environmental Science & Technology* 46 (2): 652–60.

Cairncross, S., C. Hunt, S. Boisson, K. Bostoen, V. Curtis, I. C. Fung, and W. P. Schmidt. 2010. "Water, Sanitation and Hygiene for the Prevention of Diarrhoea." *International Journal of Epidemiology* 39 (Supplement 1): i193–i205.

Caravanos, J., R. Dowling, M. M. Téllez-Rojo, A. Cantoral, R. Kobrosly, D. Estrada, M. Orjuela, S. Gualtero, B. Ericson, A. Rivera, and R. Fuller. 2014. "Blood Lead Levels in Mexico and Pediatric Burden of Disease Implications." *Annals of Global Health* 80: 269–77.

Cropper, M., and W. Oates. 1992. "Environmental Economics: A Survey." *Journal of Economic Literature* 30: 675–740.

Curtis, V., and S. Cairncross. 2003. "Effect of Washing Hands with Soap on Diarrhoea Risk in the Community: A Systematic Review." *The Lancet Infectious Diseases* 3: 275–81.

Dickie, M., and S. Gerking. 2002. "Willingness to Pay for Reduced Morbidity." Paper presented at "Economic Valuation of Health for Environmental Policy: Assessing Alternative Approaches," Orlando, FL, March 18–19.

Ejemot, R. I., J. E. Ehiri, M. M. Meremikwu, and J. A. Critchley. 2008. "Handwashing for Preventing Diarrhoea (Review)." *The Cochrane Library* (1).

Farías, P., U. Álamo-Hernández, L. Mancilla-Sánchez, J. L. Texcalac-Sangrador, L. Carrizales-Yáñez, and H. Riojas-Rodríguez. 2014. "Lead in School Children from Morelos, Mexico: Levels, Sources and Feasible Interventions." *International Journal of Environment Research and Public Health* 11 (12): 12668–82.

Fewtrell, L., R. B. Kaufmann, D. Kay, W. Enanoria, L. Haller, and J. M. Colford. 2005. "Water, Sanitation and Hygiene Interventions to Reduce Diarrhea in Less Developed Countries: A Systematic Review and Meta-Analysis." *The Lancet Infectious Diseases* 5: 42–52.

Freeman, M., M. E. Stocks, O. Cumming, A. Jeandron, J. P. Higgins, J. Wolf, A. Prüss-Ustün, S. Bonjour, P. R. Hunter, L. Fewtrell, and V. Curtis. 2014. "Hygiene and Health: Systematic Review of Handwashing Practices Worldwide and Update of Health Effects." *Tropical Medicine and International Health* 19 (8): 906–16.

INECC (Instituto Nacional de Ecología y Cambio Climático). 2014. *Informe Nacional de la Calidad del Aire 2013, México*. Mexico City: SEMARNAT/INECC. https://sinaica.inecc.gob.mx/archivo/informes/Informe2013.pdf.

Jusko, T. A., C. R. Henderson, B. P. Lanphear, D. A. Cory-Slechta, P. J. Parsons, and R. L. Canfield. 2008. "Blood Lead Concentrations < 10 ug/dL and Child Intelligence at 6 Years of Age. *Environmental Health Perspectives* 116 (2): 243–48.

Lanphear, B. P., R. Hornung, J. Khoury, K. Yolton, P. Baghurst, D. C. Bellinger, R. L. Canfield, K. N. Dietrich, R. Bornschein, T. Greene, S. J. Rothenberg, H. L. Needleman, L. Schnaas, G. Wasserman, J. Graziano, and R. Roberts. 2005. "Low-Level Environmental Lead Exposure and Children's Intellectual Functions: An International Pooled Analysis." *Environmental Health Perspectives*, 113 (7): 894–99.

Larsen, B., and J. M. Skjelvik. 2015. *Environmental Health at the Yucatán Peninsula of Mexico. A World Bank Study*. Washington, DC: World Bank.

Lim, S. S., T. Vos, A. D. Flaxman, G. Danaei, K. Shibuya, H. Adair-Rohani, M. Amann, et al. 2012. "A Comparative Risk Assessment of Burden of Disease and Injury Attributable to 67 Risk Factors and Risk Factor Clusters in 21 Regions, 1990–2010: A Systematic Analysis for the Global Burden of Disease Study 2010." *Lancet* 380 (9859): 2224–60.

Mehta, S., H. Shin, R. Burnett, T. North, and A. Cohen. 2013. "Ambient Particulate Air Pollution and Acute Lower Respiratory Infections: A Systematic Review and Implications for Estimating the Global Burden of Disease." *Air Quality, Atmosphere and Health* 6: 69–83.

Perez-Maldonado, I. N., L. G. Pruneda-Álvarez, F. Diaz-Barriga, L. E. Batres-Esquivel, F. J. Perez-Vazquez, and R. I. Martinez-Salinas. 2011. "Indoor Air Pollution in Mexico." In *The Impact of Air Pollution on Health, Economy, Environment and Agricultural Sources*, edited by

M. Khallaf. https://www.intechopen.com/books/the-impact-of-air-pollution-on-health-economy-environment-and-agricultural-sources/indoor-air-pollution-in-mexico.

Pope, C. A. III, R. T. Burnett, D. Krewski, M. Jerrett, Y. Shi, E. E. Calle, and M. J. Thun. 2009. "Cardiovascular Mortality and Exposure to Airborne Fine Particulate Matter and Cigarette Smoke: Shape of the Exposure-Response Relationship." *Circulation* 120: 941–48.

Pope, C. A. III, R. T. Burnett, M. Turner, A. Cohen, D. Krewski, M. Jerrett, S. M. Gapstur, and M. J. Thun. 2011. "Lung Cancer and Cardiovascular Disease Mortality Associated with Ambient Air Pollution and Cigarette Smoke: Shape of the Exposure-Response Relationships." *Environmental Health Perspectives* 119 (11): 1616–21.

Rabie, T., and V. Curtis. 2006. "Handwashing and Risk of Respiratory Infections: A Quantitative Systematic Review." *Tropical Medicine and International Health* 11 (3): 258–67.

Surkan, P. J., A. Zhang, F. Trachtenberg, D. B. Daniel, S. McKinlay, and D. C. Bellinger. 2007. "Neuropsychological Function in Children with Blood Lead Levels < 10 µg/dL." *NeuroToxicology* 28 (6): 1170–77.

Trejo-Acevedo, A., F. Diaz-Barriga, L. Carrizales, G. Domínguez, R. Costilla, I. Ize-Lema, M. Yarto-Ramírez. A. Gavilán-García, J. Jesús Mejía-Saavedra, and I. N. Pérez-Maldonado. 2009. "Exposure Assessment of Persistent Organic Pollutants and Metals in Mexican Children." *Chemosphere* 74 (7): 974–80.

van Donkelaar, A., R. V. Martin, R. J. Spurr, and R. T. Burnett. 2015. "High-Resolution Satellite-derived PM2.5 from Optimal Estimation and Geographically Weighted Regression over North America." *Environmental Science and Technology* 49: 10482–91.

Villalobos, M., C. Merino-Sánchez, C. Hall, J. Grieshop, M. E. Gutiérrez-Ruiz, and M. A. Handley. 2009. "Lead (II) Detection and Contamination Routes in Environmental Sources, Cookware and Home-Prepared Foods from Zimatlán, Oaxaca, Mexico." *The Science of the Total Environment* 407: 2836–44.

Waddington, H., B. Snilstveit, H. White, and L. Fewtrell. 2009. "Water, Sanitation and Hygiene Interventions to Combat Childhood Diarrhoea in Developing Countries." Synthetic Review 001, International Initiative for Impact Evaluation (3ie), New Delhi.

Wilson, C. 2003. "Empirical Evidence Showing the Relationships between Three Approaches for Pollution Control." *Environmental and Resource Economics* 24: 97–101.

World Bank. 2008. *Environmental Health and Child Survival: Epidemiology, Economics, Experiences.* A World Bank Study. Washington, DC: World Bank.

6 Leveraging Natural Capital for Socially Inclusive Growth

PASQUALE SCANDIZZO WITH CONTRIBUTIONS BY DANIELE CUFARI

INTRODUCTION

Tourism is a complex economic activity with a potentially substantial impact on the economy and the environment, both for Quintana Roo and for Mexico as a whole. Its evolution, structure and model of industrial organization can have a profound influence on economic development, the pattern of resource use and the environment. Even though it shares many characteristics with the industrial and service sectors, tourism is peculiar in its structure: it can be considered a special subset of the economy, combining many different production sectors, both of industrial and service nature. These include the organized hotel industry and restaurant business, but also infrastructure and a series of other activities that contribute to the supply of tourist services and that are either directly consumed or are incorporated into the products and services that tourists buy.

While the value chain of tourism is potentially long and complex, in many countries the multinational nature of the business has been associated with a tendency for vertical integration. In this model, the final product is conceived as an enclave of residences and entertainment for an international and affluent crowd, heavily dependent on imported goods and services.

This pattern of organization of the industry, based on large investments by multinational hotel chains, has been expanding steadily in the past 50 years and appears to have achieved impressive success in terms of sales, profits and growth. Its characteristics as a global good has insured improving standards of quality and an increasing favor with international travelers, but, at the same time, has raised a number of questions. These questions concern both the limited impact that the enclave-based, import-dependent model has on the local economy and, more poignantly, the negative effect on the environment.

Another aspect of this structure of tourism is that it has traditionally benefited—implicitly or explicitly—from domestic subsidies that other sectors do not always have. In an attempt to attract investment, local authorities have provided incentives through a variety of means to investors (such as land, subsidized services, and duty-free imports of goods needed in the industry). These subsidies may or may not be offset by other revenues to government coffers but they inevitably lead to inefficient resource allocation. Overuse of energy and water is rampant in many places of the world because of low pricing of such commodities. Another inefficiency relates to land use. Land in coastal areas that may traditionally have been left untouched under traditional use patterns has potentially high value within the tourism sector. Land in these areas is often developed at densities far above the carrying capacity of the environment and the local services that supply such areas.

The climate change debate, in particular, has focused attention on the potentially devastating effects that sea level rise may have on a great number of resources that are located in coastal areas increasingly threatened by floods and extreme weather events. Questions have also been raised on the direct environmental impacts from massive construction and invasive architecture, as well as from the infrastructural developments induced by such a concentration of land development on fragile coastal areas. Finally, the prevailing model has also been blamed for failing to link with local culture and stimulate local business, thereby promoting mass tourism as an essentially predatory activity, with no capacity to induce, through sector and employment multipliers, endogenous growth.

Counter to this traditional scenario of international tourism as a globalized commodity having no significant linkages with the local community, several alternatives have been proposed to improve the tourism industry's contribution to the national/regional economy and, at the same time, to generate more efficient patterns of resource use with regard to the environment. These alternatives are all based on the idea that a higher level of integration with the territory and its culture is necessary for tourist resorts, and that this integration must include both the widening and the deepening of the local value chain. Moreover, all of these alternatives tend to reject the traditional concentration of tourism activity on the coast, and advocate a broader policy of investment aimed to direct tourists towards the cities of the interior and other points of attraction with cultural or entertainment value.

On the whole, these alternative scenarios can be seen as an effort to identify profiles of investment with more numerous and stronger linkages between tourism, local industry and services, cultural production, and more generally, economic development. They can also be seen as attempts to identify alternative patterns of tourism as a global and local composite consumption good, by combining the traditional reception and entertainment services with more-sophisticated forms of cultural experience, respect for the environment, and the valorization of local human and non-human resources.

The alternatives suggested to the beach resort model, however, have themselves raised a number of problems. On one hand, they are generally based on broad ideas and ideological concerns, rather than on specific, concrete and economically well-founded models. This is the case, for example, of so-called *eco-tourism*, which in most of its practical applications can still be seen more as a brave attempt to tame the conflict between mass travel and the ecological balance, than as a well-defined product and business model.

On the other hand, the new models of tourism, because of their reliance on concepts such as exploration (that is, penetration into unexplored realities) and experience of alternative cultures, threaten to generate new dangers in terms of the potential disruption of environments and populations, which were relatively unaffected by the enclave type traditional model. In virtually all cases of both old and new tourist modes, the economic and social effects are unclear regarding both their predictable results and their measured outcomes. For example, this is true in Quintana Roo for the local Mayan population, which has been affected by the Cancún type of development only to the extent that it has been used to provide low-wage workers. However, the local Mayan population could be even more adversely influenced by the development of an eco-tourism with direct impact on Mayan settlements and the local rural resource base.

While the forms of eco-tourism and cultural tourism proposed appear unclear and fraught with their own dangers, the design of alternative models should also be subject to more-detailed analysis. The search of models that would be able to involve local human and nonhuman resources and stimulate endogenous, sustainable growth, in particular, is important both to evaluate the existing tourism patterns and the economic policies that could steer the industry towards modes of production that are simultaneously more efficient and more respectful of the environment as tourism's primary resource.

Identifying forms of tourism with lower leakages, higher direct and indirect effects on the economy, dynamic economies of scale, and more and stronger linkages with other economic activities thus appears to be crucial to the understanding and the definition of appropriate economic policies for the sector. In Quintana Roo, this analysis is ever more important for many reasons. They include that, in the context of the predictable environmental disruption induced by climate change, the Cancún model of tourism development does not appear to be viable any more without radical modifications.

HIGHLIGHTS OF THE METHODOLOGY

The Social Accounting Matrix (SAM) is a system of national/regional/sub-regional accounts represented in a matrix format (Stone 1962, 1981). It includes the inter-industry linkages through transactions typically found in the Input-Output (I/O) accounts and the transactions and transfers of income between different types of economic agents, such as households, government, firms, and external institutional sectors.

The SAM consists of a set of interrelated subsystems that, on the one hand, give an analytical picture of the studied economy in a particular accounting period. On the other hand, the SAM serves as an instrument for assessing the effects of changes on the particular flows represented by it (injections and linkages in the system), which might be the result of policy measures.

The SAM is a double-entry table, describing the structure of the economic system through its disaggregation in key blocks, thought as origin and destination of transaction flows. Thanks to its theoretical and methodological characteristics, it can represent the distributive and redistributive income process by including the accounts headed to the institutional sectors (households, firms, and government). Following this approach, the economic system is typically disaggregated into the following blocks:

- Primary production factors (labor and capital)
- Production sectors (agriculture, industry, services and their disaggregations)
- Households
- Firms
- Government (public administration)
- Capital Formation (public and private gross fixed investments) and
- Rest of the Country and Rest of the World.

Both the expenditures (columns) and revenues (rows) are defined for any productive and institutional sector. If data are available, any of the above blocks can be further disaggregated depending on the objective of the analysis. The SAM can be considered an extension of the traditional I/O model proposed by Leontief, which also consists of a transaction matrix and records, in quantitative terms, the exchange flows of an economic system in a specific place, for a specific period. In its usual configuration, the SAM includes the I/O matrix of the inter-mediate exchanges between production sectors, the accounts related to institutional sectors (households, firms and government), production factors (labor and capital), capital formation, and rest of the economy.

ESTIMATING A SOCIAL ACCOUNTING MATRIX TO EVALUATE ECO-SUSTAINABLE TOURISM IN QUINTANA ROO

A new "social accounting matrix" for the economy and the environment

The problem of integrating environmental and economic accounts was first addressed through the concept of "spatial and physical economy" in the works developed by: Isard (1969), Ayres and Kneese (1969), Leontief (1970) and Victor (1972). The symmetrical environmental input–output table (SEIOT) based on the Leontief methodology included emissions to the atmosphere and water, and was further developed in several more-recent contributions. From a statistical point of view, the *National Accounts System of United Nations, 1993 (NAS93)* presented for the first time a national system of accounts extended to environmental accounting, but without a specific choice on the methodology to measure and incorporate systematically the environmental effects and on which metrics to use. After many years of debate and different attempts from national and international institutions, the UN published a manual in 2003: *SEEA03 (System of Environmental and Economic Accounting)*. This guidebook offers prescriptions for collecting, and incorporating in national accounts, the costs of physical flows linked to the environment and their connection with the monetary flows associated with production activity and consumption. The manual includes the design of a hybrid SAM—called SAMEA and subsequently SEAM—that combines economic and environmental flows in an integrated set of accounts.

Based in part on SEEA03 and in part on a parallel documentation of the European Union,[1] several countries have now a set of national environmental accounts (the so-called NAMEA accounts) integrated in one or more environmental social accounting matrices. However, since most natural resources and environmental goods are strongly rooted locally, the challenge is to develop social accounting matrices that refer to sufficiently small regional and sub-regional contexts, so that the local impact of resource management and governance can be appropriately taken into account.

Several recent studies and initiatives attempt to address this problem by developing regional SAMs. For example, Scandizzo, Ferrarese, and Vezzani (2010) develop a system of SEAM for 20 regions in Italy, which are available on a website and can be utilized flexibly to study the impact of various environmental policies on the economic system. Rodriguez, Braak, and Watson (2011) propose an automated SAM that can be used at the local level to develop economic base assessments in small regions. Uwakonye, Osho, and Ajuzie (2010) present a local application of a SEAM to the Broken Bow Lake (BBL) in Oklahoma. They value the total impact of BBL and their distribution among local stakeholders by considering SEAM direct and indirect effects of returns from hydroelectric power and municipal and industrial water activities, valued at market prices, while use losses prevented and assumed equal to net income to account for output of the flood control activity. They also value output of recreation based on a net benefit per visitor-day. Usami (2008) develops a SEAM model for villages in India to analyze interactions between economic activities and natural resources, use of local water and land resources, soil degradation caused by overuse of chemical fertilizers and pesticides, and shortage of organic matter.

Tables 6.1 and 6.2 show the structure of an environmental SAM, constructed according to the UN methodology (called SEEA03 for the SAMEA or System Environmental and Economic Accounting), which accounts for both the physical flows linked to the environmental sphere, the monetary flows associated with production activity and consumption, and their connections. From an economic standpoint, the SAMEA contains a SAM in which the flows are expressed in monetary units, associated to the economic flow, or in other words, related to production activity and consumption, as well as those that refer to a subsequent distribution and redistribution of these flows. From an environment point of view, the SAMEA rows account for the flows of natural resources that the

TABLE 6.1 Structure of a social, environmental, and economic accounting matrix

SAMEA	STATE ECONOMY	REST OF THE COUNTRY/ REST OF THE WORLD ECONOMY	STATE ENVIRONMENT	REST OF THE COUNTRY/REST OF THE WORLD ENVIRONMENT
State economy	SAM: production, income, consumption, and capital formation	Net exports	Residuals by residents	Residuals by residents to rest of the country/rest of the world
State environment	Natural resources inputs	Natural resources exports	Residuals by nonresidents	
Rest of the country/ rest of the world environment	Natural resources from rest of the world			
State residuals	Residuals reabsorbed			
Rest of the country/ rest of the world residuals	Residuals reabsorbed		Cross-boundary residual inflows	Cross-boundary residual outflows

Source: Morilla 2004.
Note: SAM = social accounting matrix; SAMEA = social, environmental, and economic accounting matrix.

TABLE 6.2 Exogenous and endogenous accounts in SAMEA

SAMEA		SAM			EA
		Endogenous accounts (m)	Exogenous accounts (k)	Totals	Environmental endogenous accounts (v)
SAM	Endogenous accounts (m)	Y_m	X_{mk}	Y_m	E_{mv}
	Exogenous accounts (k)	X_{km}	X_{kk}	X_k	—
	Totals	Y_m	X_k	—	E_v
EA	Environmental endogenous accounts	R_{rr}	—	R_r	—

Source: Morilla and Llanes 2004.
Note: — = not available; EA = environmental accounts; SAM = social accounting matrix; SAMEA = social, environmental, and economic accounting matrix.

productive system uses as inputs (for example, water resources) or the reabsorbed residuals that are picked up and processed. The SAMEA columns account instead for the emissions (that is, how recycled water is picked up by nature once it has been used by the production process), household consumption, and the emission of greenhouse effect gasses.

A SAM from Quintana Roo: Field surveys and SAM parameters

A critical input in the estimation of the SAM for Quintana Roo was provided by the results of two parallel surveys conducted by a team of researchers and students from the University of Quintana Roo and the University of Rome. They concerned, respectively, the characteristics and the potential of tourist demand (both national and international), and the socioeconomic characteristics of the local Maya population, particularly with regard to its actual or potential involvement in tourism.

Key results from the tourists' sample show an interesting socioeconomic structure, that reflects a preference for the educated, and with a sufficiently balanced professional affiliation and cultural attendance profile. The attitude towards tourism appears to be characterized by a combination of minimalist tendencies ("we are doing just a vacation") with a clear preference for cultural activities related to heritage, but not excluding the accessory facilities and activities, such as nightlife, extreme sports, and adventure. However, more than 80 percent of tourists are interested in visiting the archaeological sites and carrying out activities related to them.

The tourist sample is balanced in terms of gender representation and characterized by a large prevalence of highly educated individuals (more than 79 percent university graduates—graduate or undergraduate). However, this group seemingly behaves similarly to other groups sampled from the point of view of leisure activities and experience with cultural goods. The scenario preferred is still the traditional one, with the highest proportion of the respondents (58 percent) giving their preference to the natural beauties of the coast, but with a significant proportion interested in the cultural and ecological possibilities that their visit may yield. Willingness to pay for conservation programs appears also significant and diffused, and somewhat related to the level of education, especially in the passage from university students to graduate degree holders. In general, therefore, this sample presents a tourist profile very different from the usual practitioner of mass tourism, reflecting what could be termed a parsimonious-tentative approach to ecological and cultural tourism. Survey respondents appear well educated and interested in cultural activities, judiciously favoring a more conservative, but potentially fruitful development scenario for tourism in Quintana Roo, and willing to contribute both money and efforts for its realization.

The household survey concerned all the Maya population of the state, with the higher concentration in the villages touched by tourism activities. Key findings show that most of the indigenous population is poor or very poor, with a high level of unemployment, little involvement in tourism and, when involved, with meager benefits from low-level jobs and precarious employment. Gender discrimination seems important, but gender roles and weights appear nonconventional and changing. Even though 80 percent of the men interviewed claimed that they would not allow women to work, the roles of women in the workforce and in breadwinning for the family appear significant, with little involvement in agriculture and a major presence in commerce and services. Sensitivity to ecological issues seems high and willingness to pay for a conservation programs is correspondingly high, on average, even though many of the respondents believe that conservation should be a prerogative and a responsibility of the government.

The results from the survey also suggest that the Maya individuals and communities look at tourism as a potentially very beneficial activity and that they are well inclined, and in many cases, eager, to participate in ecotourism development. However, the following could potentially constitute obstacles to developing a grassroots-based ecological tourism:

- The lack of a good health system: For instance, in the small villages, medical facilities are closed in the weekend and often also during the week
- The lack of a good educational system (most of the villages only have primary schools) and in many cases (such as in Señor) people speak only Maya
- The lack of a good transportation system (some villages can be reached only by taxi or private car, such as X-Cabil)
- The strong decision power of Farmers' Councils that decide land use and
- Gender discrimination.

Other data sources

Other data used to estimate the Quintana Roo integrated economic and environmental SAM were drawn from the following sources:

- National Account Data, including a rather aggregate estimate of make and use industrial tables
- The SAM for Mexico from the Global Trade Analysis Project database
- An estimate of the state input-output table from the University of Quintana Roo
- Data from the National Household Survey
- Time series statistics of national account, production, and consumption data
- Aggregate sector data for agriculture, tourism, infrastructure, and so forth
- Energy sector statistics and
- Environmental statistics.

The SAM estimated

Existing data, together with primary data collected by the two field surveys, were used both to construct the SAM and as baseline inputs to define the alternative scenarios of tourism development and climate change. The constructed SAM (table 6.3 presents a simplified version) has 29 sectors[2] and is calibrated to the year 2010.

The results show a rather sparse matrix, indicating an economy characterized by high import dependence and low linkages between sectors, including the main drivers of development, such as tourism, construction, industry and government services. Table 6.4 and figure 6.1 show the values of forward and backward linkages. Forward linkages measure the capacity of a sector, as compared to the average, to participate in a general increase of the whole economy. In turn, backward linkages measure the capacity of a sector, as compared to the average, to generate a diffused increase in the rest of the economy. More specifically, the forward linkage measures the average increase in a sector's activity level

TABLE 6.3 Structure of the Quintana Roo social accounting matrix

	SECTORS	INSTITUTIONS	FACTORS	CAPITAL FORMATION	NATURAL CAPITAL FORMATION	NATURAL RESOURCES	TOTAL
Sectors	Intermediate input costs (intermediate demand = intermediate supply)	Final good expenditures (final demand)	n.a.	Capital goods produced	Natural capital creation or destruction	n.a.	Total demand = total supply
Institutions	Taxes and other transfers	Transfers	Factor income = payments to households	n.a.	n.a.	Payments to institutions (for example, to capital formation)	Total institutional incomes = total institutional expenditures
Factors (value added)	Factor income	n.a.	n.a.	n.a.	n.a.	n.a.	n.a.
Capital formation	n.a.	Savings	n.a.	n.a.	n.a.	n.a.	n.a.
Natural capital formation	n.a.	Natural capital savings (or depletion)	n.a.	n.a.	n.a.	n.a.	n.a.
Natural resources	Natural resource costs (private and social)	Natural resource expenditures (private and social)	n.a.	n.a.	n.a.	n.a.	Total resource receipts (costs + expenditures)= Total benefits to institutions

Note: n.a. = not applicable.

TABLE 6.4 Quintana Roo SAM: Rasmussen indexes of forward and backward linkages

	FORWARD	BACKWARD
Value added	4.459184	1.183456
Biodiversity forest	0.429921	1.042357
Biodiversity wetland	0.304789	1.05221
Agriculture, livestock, harness. forestry, fishing, and hunting	0.539219	1.03714
Mining	0.229056	1.113386
Electricity, water, and gas supply	0.846716	1.245628
Construction	0.249896	1.247241
Manufacturing industries	0.852202	0.438523
Commerce	1.426691	1.112236
Transportation, mail, and storage	0.996324	0.89679
Information in mass media	0.55035	1.162402
Financial and insurance services	0.248309	0.396616
Real estate services (of movable and intangible assets)	1.316143	0.614122
Professional, scientific, and technical services	0.373117	1.051363
Support services for business and waste management	1.263541	1.071912
Educational services	0.569783	0.896439
Health and social assistance services	0.349011	0.797104

(continued)

TABLE 6.4, *continued*

	FORWARD	BACKWARD
Recreational, cultural, sports, related services	0.410275	1.20214
Temporary accommodations, and food and drink preparation	2.519568	1.093525
Other services, except government activities	0.46917	0.80671
Government activities	0.369899	1.083864
Public administration	2.006272	0.779063
Tourists who are residents	0.562416	1.175167
Indigenous families	0.535554	1.012209
Non-indigenous families	4.744519	1.01782
Foreign tourists	0.18197	1.21531
Natural capital	0.196107	1.255267

FIGURE 6.1

Forward and backward linkages

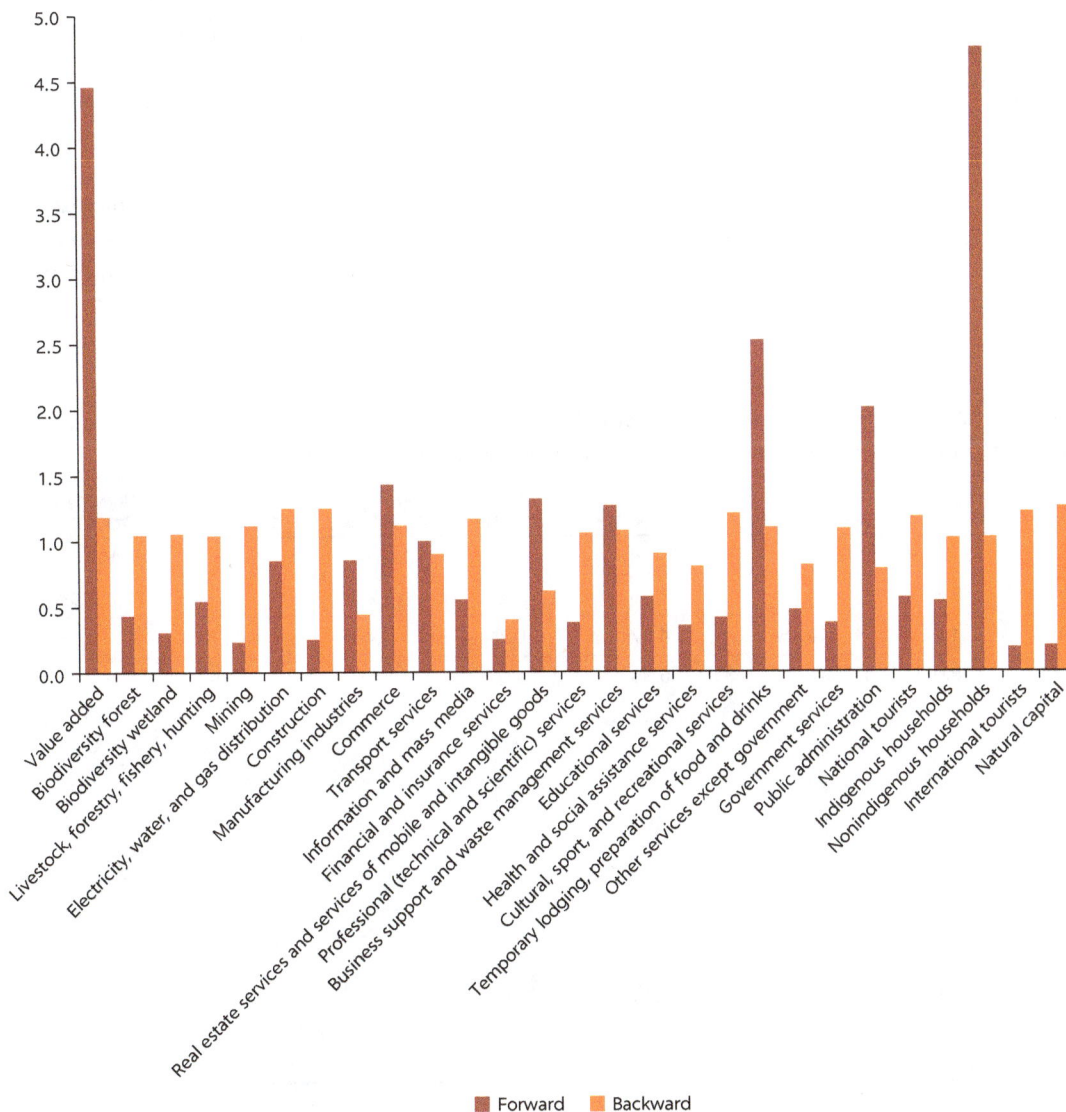

■ Forward ■ Backward

(output or income) resulting from a unit increase in all sectors' output. The backward linkage measures the increase in the average output of all sectors resulting from a unit increase of the activity level of the sector considered. In both cases, the measure is transformed into a Rasmussen Index by dividing its values for the overall forward or backward linkage average.

As the analyses show, forward linkages are lower than the average for productive and many service sectors, but high for some sectors that are linked to traditional tourism, such as hotels and restaurants. However, they are relatively high for value added from factor income and non-indigenous households, implying a relatively high degree of inclusion of domestic labor and capital, and residents in the economy. Indigenous households, on the other hand, seem to have a very low degree of participation in the market economy, with very high level of exclusion in terms of upstream activities, such as employment in tourism, transportation and other more dynamic market activities. Backward linkages, which measure the capacity of each sector to generate positive spillovers for the economy, are somewhat larger and exceed unity for both domestic and international tourists.

Tables 6.5 and 6.6 show the impact multiplier estimates. These can be interpreted as the result of several policy experiments, where the impact on all sectors and institutions is computed (along the columns) in response to an exogenous increase in each sector activity or institution of 100 units of production (for sectors) or income (for institutions). The exogenous increases in sector production can be interpreted as increases in corresponding sector demands, while institutions' income increases can be interpreted as increases in remittances from the rest of the country or the rest of the world (including subsidies), productivity, or employment shocks. For tourists, income increases correspond to increases in preferences (greater number of tourists) for Quintana Roo and increased willingness to pay per tourist or both. Table 6.5, which reports the values of the

TABLE 6.5 Quintana Roo social accounting matrix impact multipliers: Percentage increases in production and income from an injection in employment and demand for goods and services

	LABOR AND CAPITAL	AGRICULTURE	CONSTRUCTION	INDUSTRY	COMMERCE	DOMESTIC TOURISTS	INTERNATIONAL TOURISTS
Value added	184.91	94.55	127.24	32.74	121.88	100.72	104.61
Biodiversity forest	3.59	25.24	8.95	1.52	2.87	8.24	7.93
Biodiversity wetland	1.84	13.25	4.67	0.79	1.46	4.28	4.14
Agriculture, forestry, and fishery	8.01	115.18	6.89	4.91	6.26	5.19	5.19
Construction	1.15	0.95	103.30	0.27	1.01	0.96	0.94
Industry	39.82	27.86	36.65	109.82	34.39	31.34	33.90
Commerce and other services	221.23	158.41	247.87	62.12	296.62	290.93	304.76
Government	43.45	51.39	53.25	10.67	53.13	36.83	37.40
Indigenous households	8.22	9.78	9.62	1.96	9.32	6.82	6.92
Non-indigenous households	172.75	106.18	127.34	31.69	119.76	100.12	103.49
Natural capital	0.74	0.62	0.69	0.15	0.67	0.86	0.52

multipliers in response to shocks in employment, sector activities, and tourism, suggests that the greatest impact is always obtained on the service sector, with the maximum (340 percent of the shock) obtained from the increase in the income from international tourists. The largest overall impact (on value added) is from employment (184 percent), followed by an increase in the activity level of the construction sector and of commerce, which would cause value added to increase by 127 percent and 121 percent, respectively. As mentioned earlier, the indigenous population benefits only marginally (if at all) from any of these expansions, which are mainly appropriated by the non-indigenous population and the government.

Table 6.6 shows the values of similar multipliers, but with the exogenous stimulus applied directly to the institutions, among which is included natural capital (or *Mother Nature*) as a sector that represents natural resources and related activities. An increase in the value of this sector has indeed the highest multiplier (104 percent) on value added, and a very high one on services (199 percent) and on non-indigenous households (107 percent). This is a somewhat surprising result, and is mainly due to the importance of this form of capital in Quintana Roo for activities such as forestry, fishery, energy and water supply, and even construction and industry. The result also implies that any deterioration of natural resources due to overexploitation and poor conservation practices would have large negative consequences for the state economy. The table also shows that, while the effect of an exogenous income increase of household income on value added is of the same order of magnitude for both indigenous (82 percent) and non-indigenous (86 percent) families, the latter are able to appropriate a much larger share of any direct income increases. Only for an income subsidy paid directly to them, as in the case of the *Prospera* program, are the indigenous households able to claim a benefit slightly above 100 percent of the income transfer. In all other cases, the forward multiplier, which measures their participation in the case of growing income for government, other households, or natural capital, is under 10 percent.

TABLE 6.6 Impact multipliers: Percentage increases in production and income from an injection in income of institutions and natural capital

	GOVERNMENT	INDIGENOUS HOUSEHOLDS	NON-INDIGENOUS HOUSEHOLDS	NATURAL CAPITAL
Value added	55.88	82.04	85.66	103.65
Biodiversity forest	2.77	5.82	3.28	12.85
Biodiversity wetland	1.39	3.02	1.68	6.73
Agriculture, forestry, and fishery	6.65	21.38	8.21	48.78
Construction	1.26	1.17	1.16	22.02
Industry	22.02	37.67	41.64	71.77
Commerce and other services	140.05	205.56	221.47	198.83
Government	122.55	42.28	38.75	50.26
Indigenous households	19.88	107.46	6.82	9.15
Non-indigenous households	78.26	83.96	185.09	107.97
Natural capital	1.04	0.73	0.71	100.62

POLICY ANALYSIS: DEVELOPMENT SCENARIOS

Three scenarios were developed with the SAM, each representing a different strategy of tourism and economic development. For each scenario, a simulation was carried out to estimate the impact of alternative investment patterns. The three scenarios are: (a) Business as Usual (BAU), (b) Focused Growth, and (c) National Expansion.

The BAU scenario reflects the most recent features of tourism in Quintana Roo, which can be characterized as slow increases in demand and supply of the traditional forms of tourism. Tourist expenses tend to decline and mass tourism negatively affects natural resources (wetland and forests) by exploiting the ecosystem services, without contributing to conservation and restoration of natural capital. From the point of view of the rest of the economy, this scenario is characterized by unchanged production and a slow decrease in value added.

The Focused Growth scenario reflects an increase in mass tourism, with a massive development of resorts and the associated negative effects on ecosystem services. The growth in the tourism sector is characterized by foreign tourism, according to the traditional pattern, which is essentially based on imports. On the economic development side, there is a slow increase in productivity and in jobs for the local population. Tourist expenses decrease significantly and households' consumption slightly decreases.

The National Expansion scenario reflects an economic development focusing on investment in sustainable tourism, family hotels, and environmentally healthy, inclusive, and resilient growth. Investments are projected to enhance small, local enterprises. Tourism expansion is combined with the development of the local value chain, with lower contributions from imports. The sustainable character of this type of tourism supports the development of ecosystem services, with an increase in wetland and forest conservation. The rest of the economy is characterized by significant increases in local jobs and services supply, with increases also in tourist expenses and households' consumption capacity (table 6.7).

TABLE 6.7 **Alternative scenarios**

SCENARIO	FOCUSED GROWTH		BUSINESS AS USUAL		NATIONAL EXPANSION	
	QUALITATIVE	QUANTITATIVE (%)	QUALITATIVE	QUANTITATIVE (%)	QUALITATIVE	QUANTITATIVE (%)
Tourism						
Resort and grand hotel	Many more	100	Slow increase	15	No increase-rehabilitation	20
Family hotel	Growth	30	Slow increase	15	Many more	100
Tourists	Increase	30	Slight increase	15	Increase	50
Visitors to attractions other than beaches	No growth	0	No growth	0	Strongly encouraged	50
Road construction	Increase		Slight increase		Better maintenance	
Environment and biodiversity						
Wetland	Decrease	−50	Decrease	−50	Slight increase	10
Forest	Decrease	−50	Decrease	−50	Slight increase	10
Corals	Decrease	−30	Decrease	−30	Slight increase	10
Carbon stored	Decrease	−30	Decrease/stable	−10	Increase	30

(continued)

TABLE 6.7, *continued*

SCENARIO	FOCUSED GROWTH		BUSINESS AS USUAL		NATIONAL EXPANSION	
	QUALITATIVE	QUANTITATIVE (%)	QUALITATIVE	QUANTITATIVE (%)	QUALITATIVE	QUANTITATIVE (%)
Production and economy						
Benefits to communities around tourist places	No change	0	No change	0	Increase	10
					Education and health	25
Jobs for locals	Slight increase	20	Steady decline	−5	Significant increase	40
Jobs around other Mexican NPs	No change	0	Steady decline	−5	Significant increase	40
Tourist expenses per capita	Decrease	−25	Decrease	−25	Increase	10
Intermediate imports	Slow increase	5	Increase	15	Decrease	−20
Export	Increase in tourism	70	Slow increase in tourism	5	Increase in tourism	70
	Slow increase in manufacture	10			Slow increase in other economic sector	10
Economic production	No change	0	Slow decrease	−5	No change	0
Value added	Slow increase	3	Slow decrease	−3	Increase	20
Household consumption	Slow decrease	−5	Slow decrease	−5	Increase	13

To simulate the structural effects of the policies embedded in the different scenarios, a differential reformulation of the linear (Leontief) Input-Output model was used, according to the following equation:

$$\Delta X = (I-A^*)^{-1}[(\Delta A)X + \Delta Y] \qquad (6.1)$$

Where A and A* are the SAM matrices, respectively, with and without the scenarios' hypotheses, and ΔY is the vector of exogenous changes in receipts or expenditure of the capital account (project intervention or exogenous investment). The hypothetical conditions characterizing each scenario and the effect of the same investment program within each scenario (table 6.8) are then explored, through a SAM simulation according to equation 6.1. While the change in the SAM matrix is different for each scenario, the investment program is the same and includes a direct transfer to households, of US$570 million, with the expenditure vector based on several types of investment projects in the tourism and environmental sectors.

As the results show, each scenario has significantly different implications, resulting in widely different impacts of the investments made for families, national tourists, and biodiversity, among other sectors.

Table 6.9 shows the structural shocks resulting from changes in the production and behavioral coefficients associated with the different scenarios. While the results in table 6.9 are independent of a particular investment program and illustrate the overall impact of structural changes postulated for the three scenarios above, they have an impact on the investment program through the changes in the coefficients and linkages reflected in the SAM model. Table 6.10

TABLE 6.8 Investment impact by scenario (US$, millions)

	SHOCK	FOCUSED GROWTH	BAU	NATIONAL EXPANSION
Value added	0	336.89	360.62	440.68
Biodiversity forest	120	144.02	138.65	163.08
Biodiversity wetland	120	132.23	129.74	142.34
Agriculture, livestock, forestry, fisheries, and hunting	0	52.46	48.53	65.32
Mining	0	0.071	0.10	0.087
Electricity, water, and gas supply	0	67.26	72.70	79.19
Construction	0	6.48	4.39	6.44
Manufacturing industry	0	90.54	92.85	107.83
Commerce	0	52.32	3.16	171.55
Transport, mail, and storage	0	103.85	68.20	114.63
Mass media	0	40.43	48.80	47.64
Financial and insurance services	0	11.22	126.66	10.69
Real estate services	0	137.71	145.35	155.35
Professional, scientific, and technical services	0	31.70	28.91	32.03
Business support and waste management services	0	114.69	125.52	122.96
Education services	0	65.88	57.95	54.85
Health and social services	0	27.118	24.86	27.082
Recreational, cultural, and sports services	30	52.83	52.87	54.89
Lodging, food, and beverage preparation	0	293.56	266.62	344.50
Other services (excluding government activities)	0	40.69	40.43	44.56
Government activities	0	36.15	31.67	29.50
Public administration	80	445.81	447.09	397.53
Resident tourists	0	58.51	45.02	71.76
Indigenous families	140	196.29	189.69	225.96
Non-indigenous families	80	443.03	528.65	665.32

Note: BAU = Business as usual.

TABLE 6.9 Impact of structural changes (US$, millions)

	BAU	FOCUSED GROWTH	NATIONAL EXPANSION
Value added	6,556.01	5,233.87	10,279.80
Biodiversity forest	−3,979.15	−3,110.64	3,067.43
Biodiversity wetland	−2,075.50	−1,675.09	1,582.12
Agriculture, livestock, forestry, fisheries, and hunting	−226.53	488.71	2,454.92
Mining	24.85	1.46	114.13
Electricity, water, and gas supply	4,184.59	697.51	4,571.59
Construction	−515.77	509.16	2,670.80
Manufacturing industry	1,775.90	3,157.33	−2,990.76
Commerce	−64,367.49	−38,627.10	1,787.49

(continued)

TABLE 6.9, *continued*

	BAU	FOCUSED GROWTH	NATIONAL EXPANSION
Transport, mail, and storage	−11,371.37	5,611.62	−709.34
Mass media	5,140.96	2,162.67	−1,943.54
Financial and insurance services	55,176.01	439.72	−683.87
Real estate services	4,287.56	1,374.32	−10,144.01
Professional, scientific, and technical services	2,066.87	3,254.89	−644.25
Business support and waste management services	10,664.17	1,408.56	195.10
Education services	−1,863.71	4,879.52	1,371.06
Health and social services	62.81	2,361.89	260.76
Recreational, cultural, and sports services	1,275.60	1,746.94	911.20
Lodging, food, and beverage preparation	16,667.83	35,167.54	25,728.35
Other services (excluding government activities)	1,390.99	1,855.43	−1,913.52
Government activities	283.78	3,184.64	470.32
Public administration	11,408.12	−5,669.22	−8,155.54
Resident tourists	331.55	5,193.04	3,613.92
Indigenous families	−13,709.34	−8,190.18	5,265.36
Non-indigenous families	3,280.78	−21,474.38	1,762.64

Note: BAU = Business as usual.

TABLE 6.10 Total impact (US$, millions)

$\Delta X = (I − A^*)^{-1}[(\Delta A)X + \Delta Y] =$				$(I − A^*)^{-1}(\Delta A)X$			+	$(I − A^*)^{-1} \times \Delta Y$	
	BAU	FOCUSED GROWTH	NATIONAL EXPANSION	BAU	FOCUSED GROWTH	NATIONAL EXPANSION	BAU	FOCUSED GROWTH	NATIONAL EXPANSION
Value added	−8,786.21	5,153.93	56,591.37	−8,857.50	5,054.01	56,333.86	71.29	99.92	257.51
Biodiversity forest	−3,980.95	−2,387.52	7,029.83	−4,015.26	−2,426.93	6,968.35	34.31	39.41	61.49
Biodiversity wetland	−2,024.56	−1,277.78	3,671.50	−2,059.80	−1,315.36	3,622.24	35.25	37.58	49.26
Agriculture, livestock, forestry, fisheries, and hunting	−2,877.75	−1,911.81	6,581.96	−2,885.16	−1,925.27	6,547.30	7.41	13.47	34.67
Mining	24.17	2.57	133.00	24.12	2.55	132.67	0.05	0.02	0.33
Electricity, water, and gas supply	3,308.43	3,961.90	3,999.17	3,287.88	3,942.22	3,965.65	20.55	19.68	33.52
Construction	−618.43	395.42	3,748.21	−618.78	392.67	3,737.99	0.35	2.75	10.22
Manufacturing industry	−1,479.17	−767.26	4,831.36	−1,499.25	−791.33	4,787.56	20.08	24.08	43.80
Commerce	−64,638.06	−42,052.54	18,123.45	−64,524.98	−41,993.10	18,025.02	−113.08	−59.44	98.42
Transport, mail, and storage	−13,967.78	2,688.41	9,434.84	−13,958.45	2,655.62	9,376.68	−9.33	32.79	58.17

(continued)

TABLE 6.10, *continued*

	BAU	FOCUSED GROWTH	NATIONAL EXPANSION	BAU	FOCUSED GROWTH	NATIONAL EXPANSION	BAU	FOCUSED GROWTH	NATIONAL EXPANSION
Mass media	3,568.74	1,571.17	2,352.08	3,552.06	1,559.83	2,331.53	16.68	11.34	20.56
Financial and insurance services	50,852.28	194.18	104.29	50,733.02	190.36	100.82	119.26	3.82	3.47
Real estate services	29,18.81	4,656.73	4,797.23	2,879.72	4,618.01	4,739.48	39.09	38.73	57.75
Professional, scientific, and technical services	64.57	1,615.69	1,713.46	56.87	1,603.82	1,700.06	7.70	11.86	13.40
Business support and waste management services	13,627.34	12,041.19	16,926.93	13,579.45	12,001.40	16,853.71	47.89	39.79	73.21
Education services	−1,297.84	3,552.16	4,766.05	−1,315.77	3,524.05	4,740.58	17.93	28.12	25.47
Health and social services	−433.93	1,266.35	2,286.47	−440.03	1,256.76	2,272.97	6.10	9.59	13.50
Recreational, cultural, and sports services	1,840.62	3,038.65	3,989.00	1,823.22	3,018.58	3,964.43	17.39	20.07	24.57
Lodging, and food and beverage preparation	20,023.29	48,404.13	57,385.11	19,934.05	48,280.97	57,178.94	89.24	123.17	206.17
Other services (excluding government activities)	32.61	737.28	1,554.88	22.65	725.15	1,537.98	9.96	12.13	16.89
Government activities	164.96	2,474.01	1,747.29	154.28	2,457.85	1,735.88	10.69	16.16	11.41
Public administration	−12,682.20	−16,684.51	11,651.86	−12,836.25	−16,842.68	11,531.86	154.05	158.17	120.00
Resident tourists	−841.98	4,478.01	8,778.97	−850.68	4,456.42	8,741.69	8.70	21.59	37.27
Indigenous families	−15,077.64	−10,242.76	8,452.23	−15,115.58	−10,293.76	8,372.03	37.94	50.99	80.19
Non-indigenous families	−8,087.89	−19,664.58	58,614.87	−8,178.90	−19,727.88	58,264.09	91.01	63.30	350.78

Note: BAU = Business as usual.

sums up the total impact divided into medium impact and investment impact for each scenario, according to equation 6.1.

The impact of the structural changes shown in table 6.9 suggests a number of considerations. A move to the National Expansion scenario appears to perform best in terms of productivity (value added increase) and is the only change that does not have an adverse effect on biodiversity and that does increase the incomes of local residents, including poorer indigenous households. In addition, this structural transformation seems to be consistent with an economic expansion based on agriculture, construction, and tourism, somewhat at the expense of manufacturing and other capital-intensive activities, such as transportation. These results are confirmed by considering the effects of structural changes combined with an injection of exogenous resources (table 6.10). In the case examined, the move to the National Expansion scenario performs far better than the changes to the other two scenarios from the perspective of income generation, income distribution, environmental protection, and tourism promotion.

SUMMARY

This chapter has provided an applied analysis of the various economic, social, and environmental linkages that exist in a small open economy such as Quintana Roo. Using selected primary survey techniques and existing structural models of the local economy, the extended SAM model estimated permits simulation of development scenarios using controlled assumptions. Such analyses can also be conducted for other states in the Yucatán, or the general lessons can be extrapolated and tested in less quantitative terms through focus groups or targeted surveys. Most notably, the modeling efforts demonstrate that viable alternatives exist to traditional tourism models. Specifically, a *National Expansion* scenario contemplates tourism expansion combined with the development of a local value chain, with lower contributions from imports. It results in increases in value added, and is the only scenario evaluated that does not have an adverse effect on biodiversity and that does increase the incomes of local residents, including poorer indigenous households. In brief, the scenario performs best from the perspective of income generation, income distribution, environmental protection, and tourism promotion. Such scenario analyses are a powerful tool in setting priorities and in identifying appropriate policy interventions in the context of coastal management and planning.

NOTES

1. The first document of the EU in this regard is a 1994 position paper by the European Commission, titled "Directions for the European Union on Environmental Indicators and ... Integration of Economic and Environmental Information Systems."
2. The sectors are Agriculture and fishing (1 sector); Industry (4 sectors); Services (13 sectors); Value Added (Labor and Capital); Institutions: indigenous (Maya) households, nonindigenous households, domestic tourists, government, and international tourists; Investment and saving; Natural Capital; and Rest of the World.

REFERENCES

Ayres, R. U., and A. V. Kneese. 1969. "Production, Consumption and Externalities." *American Economic Review* 59: 282–97.

Isard, W. 1969. *General Theory: Social, Political, Economic, and Regional, with Particular Reference to Decision-Making Analysis.* Cambridge, MA: MIT Press.

Leontief, W. 1970. "Environmental Repercussions and the Economic Structure: An Input-Output Approach." *Review of Economic Statistics* 52: 262–77.

Morilla, C. R., 2004. "Sistema híbrido para el análisis de las relaciones entre el medioambiente, la economía y la sociedad: aplicación para año 2000, al recurso agua y las emisiones a la atmósfera en España." Unpublished Ph.D. Dissertation. University of Sevilla.

Morilla, C. R., and G. Llanes. 2004. "Multiplicadores domésticos SAMEA en un modelo mutisectorial ecoambiental de la economía española." Working Paper FEDEA (eee184). http://www.fedea.es.

Rodriguez, A., P. Watson, and W. Braak. 2011. "Getting to Know the Economy in Your Community: Automated Social Accounting." *Journal of Extension* 49 (4).

Scandizzo, P. L., C. Ferrarese, and A. Vezzani. 2010. "La Matrice di Contabilità Sociale, una nuova metodologia di stima" (The Social Accounting Matrix: A New Estimation Methodology). *Il Risparmio* 58 (3): 19–63.

Stone, R. N. 1962. "Multiple Classifications in Social Accounting." *Bulletin de l'Institut International de Statistique* 39 (3): 215–33.

——. 1981. "The Relationship of Demographic Accounts to National Income and Product Accounts." In *Social Accounting Systems, Essays on the State of the Art*, edited by F. T. Juster and K. C. Land. New York: Academic Press.

Usami, Y. 2008. "A Note on Construction of a Regional Social Accounting Matrix with Natural Resource Accounts: Linking Village/Industry Level Data to Regional Level Studies." Osaka: Osaka Prefecture University.

Uwakonye, M. N., G. S. Osho, and E. I. S. Ajuzie. 2010. "The Economic Impact of Water Resource: Broken Bow Lake in McCurtain County in Southeastern Oklahoma." *Journal of Business & Economic Research* 8 (4): 63–76.

Victor, P. A. 1972. *Pollution: Economy and Environment*. London, UK: George Allen and Unwin Ltd.

7 Environmental Impact Assessment for Integrated Coastal Zone Management

ERNESTO-SÁNCHEZ-TRIANA, SANTIAGO ENRIQUEZ, AND
KATHARINA SIGMANN

INTRODUCTION

The following chapter seeks to analyze how the Mexican Environmental Impact Assessment (EIA) process could contribute to integrated coastal zone management and environmentally sustainable development in coastal and shoreline zones. To that end, the general EIA process in Mexico will be described shortly, followed by an analysis of recently carried out case studies in priority sites of the state of Campeche.[1] The chapter closes with a discussion on potential reforms to the EIA system.

EIA IN MEXICO

Latin American countries have used EIA as an environmental management tool to "control the environmental impacts of a broad range of projects" (Sánchez-Triana and Enriquez 2007) "Through EIA, authorities often establish design and operation conditions that aim to compensate for the lack of adequate environmental standards" (Sánchez-Triana and Enriquez 2007). In the region, the responsibility for environmental compliance falls on project developers, who must meet EIA-related requirements that are evaluated and enforced by the relevant government authority. The preparation of EIAs is mandatory for specific actions, usually referred to as projects, activities, or works, among others.

In this regard, Mexico is no exception.[2] The overall objective of Mexico's EIA system is to avoid or reduce negative impacts by setting conditions for infrastructure projects or activities that could disrupt ecological balance, or violate established limits and conditions, as set out in the General Law of Ecological Equilibrium and Environmental Protection and its regulations.[3] Hence, EIA is about identifying the potential environmental effects or impacts of a proposed action, and identifying the necessary corrective or mitigation measures.

The law and regulations of Mexico contain a list of actions that require an EIA, as well as the characteristics, circumstances, thresholds, and additional aspects that would trigger the preparation of an EIA for such actions.

These instruments also contemplate special types of constructions and activities that are excluded by the regulations and therefore by law do not require an EIA.

The supervision of the EIA process is the responsibility of the federal environmental ministry—SEMARNAT. State and municipal authorities can request the preparation of EIAs for activities that are not explicitly considered as a responsibility of the Federal government. In addition, the Federal government can sign agreements with states or municipalities, transferring them responsibilities for various environmental management responsibilities, including EIA. This is a logical consequence of the conception of EIA as an environmental management tool, which is consistent with the perception of EIA in the region as a whole.

There are two types of Environmental Impact Statement (Manifestación de Impacto Ambiental—MIA): Regional and Particular. Regional MIAs apply to actions with potential regional effects, such as industrial parks, highways and railways, or projects that would affect a watershed or lead in any way to the destruction, isolation or fragmentation of ecosystems. The Particular MIA is for actions triggering an EIA that do not qualify for a Regional MIA. A MIA must be complemented by a risk study if the action is considered as a high risk. Actions may be exempted from the EIA if the foreseen impacts are already regulated by norms, the works or activities are expressly contemplated in a regional development or urban development plan approved by SEMARNAT, or if the facilities will be located within authorized industrial parks. In such cases, the developer must prepare a Preventive Report (Informe Preventivo—IP).

In addition, there is no formal scoping procedure. The EIA scope generally includes consideration of ecosystems, their preservation and restoration, and protection of the environment. Environmental forecasts, and identification, description, and evaluation of the following impacts must be presented: environmental, cumulative, synergistic, significant or relevant, and residual. Local and regional MIA must include environmental projections and evaluation of alternatives. The legal framework requires the definition of mitigation measures as part of the EIA, but does not call for a structured plan or program to ensure that such measures are systematically integrated into the action's operation. Specific MIAs must include measures to prevent and mitigate impacts. Regional MIA must include strategies to prevent and mitigate impacts (cumulative and residual) on the regional environment.

The law states that the authorization of works and activities must consider compliance with legal requirements, urban development and regional development plans, and the existence of natural protected areas. This is particularly important when it comes to local ecological programs (see chapter 2), which must be considered if they have been adopted through the official publication of a decree from the Executive Power of the corresponding jurisdiction.

Any individual can prepare IP and MIA. Specifically, there is no need to consult with a registered or specialized firm to elaborate the MIA.

SEMARNAT is required by the law to notify state and local governments when it receives MIAs for hazardous or radioactive waste facilities, industrial parks where high-risk activities will be undertaken, real estate developments that will affect coastal ecosystems, or actions that will affect natural protected areas under federal jurisdiction. As part of the evaluation of the MIA, SEMARNAT may request the technical opinion of other public agencies or entities, if required by the type of work or activity. However, no concrete rules or procedures are established for these additional consultations.

SEMARNAT publishes weekly lists of IP and MIAs. Thus, as well as the MIA itself, the files of the respective MIAs are available to the public. Action developers may request the classification of information that, if disclosed, could affect industrial property rights or commercial interests. Public consultations are only carried out under specific circumstances, and specifically only based on a decision by SEMARNAT whether to carry out a consultation or not and following a request by a member of an affected community. In special cases, public meetings are held for information and feedback.

Finally, the Federal Environmental Attorney (PROFEPA) must inspect and monitor compliance with regulations and environmental authorizations. PROFEPA can require responsible parties to present information on compliance with environmental provisions.

EIA IN COASTAL ZONES

MIAs follow the general rules and procedures established by the law and regulations regarding those terms. For the purpose of this analysis, two field sides in the state of Campeche were chosen—a tourist and fishery coastal area, Sabancuy and one of the Yucatán Peninsula's most important ports, Seybaplaya.

The EIAs presented for these regions during the last 10 years were consulted. Those that specifically referred to interventions on the shoreline were thoroughly analyzed. EIAs for projects inland, offshore, or with no implication to the shoreline—such as developments within the port—were excluded from the analysis. The case studies are based on the MIAs for three projects in Sabancuy and two projects in Seybaplaya that aim at

a) Dredging of the channel that connects Sabancuy with the Gulf of Mexico to assure secure waterways for fishermen and ships;

b) Avoiding coastal erosion in the intervention zone through hard infrastructure; and

c) Interventions to the port, including land reclamation and breakwaters.

Specifically, in the case of dredging projects, the commercial use of the dredged materials was explicitly mentioned in the EIAs, highlighting the commercial interest associated with this activity. SEMARNAT approved all MIAs. Thus, they provide an opportunity to evaluate if the projects achieved their overall objectives, and to evaluate whether and how the projects contributed to sustainable shoreline development. The results of the analysis shed light on the potential role of EIA as an integrated coastal zone management (ICZM) tool.

The main results of the analysis are outlined below.

Regional vs. specific MIA

Beside the provision in the legal framework for regional MIAs, all proponents presented specific project-based MIAs for their interventions. Table 7.1 shows the differences in the content of regional and specific MIAs. However, it can be assumed that specifically the definition of the environmental system would be quite different considering a regional rather than a specific MIA. Logically, the definition of the environmental systems leads to different perspectives on environmental problems, possible project impacts, and even the applicable legal instruments on territory and urban planning.

TABLE 7.1 Comparison of specific and regional MIA content

#	SPECIFIC MIA	REGIONAL MIA
1	General project data, information regarding the proponent, and those responsible for the environmental impact study	General project data, information regarding the proponent, and those responsible for the environmental impact study
2	Project description	Description of works or activities and, where appropriate, programs or development plans
3	Linkages with applicable legal environmental instruments and, if applicable, with land use regulation	Compliance with planning instruments and applicable laws and regulations
4	Description of the environmental system and indication of any environmental problems detected in the project's influence zone	Description of the regional environmental system and description of trends in regional development and deterioration
5	Identification, description, and evaluation of environmental impacts	Identification, description, and evaluation of the environmental, cumulative and residual impacts of the regional environmental system
6	Prevention and mitigation measures for environmental impacts	Prevention and mitigation strategies for the environmental, cumulative, and residual impacts of the regional environmental system
7	Environmental forecast and, if applicable, evaluation of alternatives	Environmental forecast and, if applicable, evaluation of alternatives
8	Identification of methodological instruments and technical elements that support the information indicated in the previous sections	Identification of methodological instruments and technical elements that support the results of the environmental impact statement

Source: Based on http://www.semarnat.gob.mx/temas/gestion-ambiental/impacto-ambiental-y-tipos/contenido-de-una-mia.
Note: MIA = Manifestación de Impacto Ambiental.

Considering that Campeche's coast lacks a regional POEGT (chapter 2 provides more details), there seems to be no regional focus when it comes to interventions on the coastline. The same can be assumed for Quintana Roo, where only the region of Sian Ka'an, a national protected area, is covered by a regional POEGT. Only Yucatán state presents a statewide regional coastal POEGT. While it is assumed that such regional POEGT contributes to an ICZM focus, a specific analysis should be carried out to prove that assumption.

Currently, regional MIAs are only required for 11 categories of projects, which include industrial or aquaculture parks, aquaculture farms of more than 500 hectares, and specific types of infrastructure (dams, nuclear power plants, roads, and railways). Regional MIAs are also required for projects that might alter watersheds; for POEGTs and PDUs; and for groups, projects, or activities that would be developed in a determined ecological region. In addition, a regional MIA would be required for projects that would be developed in sites where cumulative, synergistic, or residual impacts are likely and could result in the destruction, isolation, or fragmentation of ecosystems. Available information suggests that projects developed in coastal areas would fall under the last category, but that SEMARNAT has only required project developers to elaborate project-based (specific) MIAs.

Environmental system and scope of data analyzed to determine environmental impact

The analysis showed that while the MIAs referred to the same geographic area, the environmental system described in each of them was very different. This appears to be a result of the lack of specific guidelines or requirements that project developers need to adhere to when describing the environmental system for the intervention zone.

In addition, the identification, description, and evaluation of the environmental impacts expected from the proposed project were carried out mostly based on regional data and existing sources. This is a cause of concern, particularly as all MIAs were presented as specific, and not regional, MIAs. None of the project developers gathered specific in situ data. Hence, the underlying data regarding climate, geomorphology, tide, wind, waves, flora, and fauna, among others, are rather general and taken from existing studies and sources. Table 7.2 indicates the detailed analysis of the data presented for the MIAs.

Project developers do not report—prior to project implementation or as a long-term monitoring measure—the installation of any oceanographic equipment that would measure the daily variation in sea level, wind, waves and/or currents. Neither do they gather specific field data to quantify the variation in the characteristics of the sand and the respective beach profiles.

As mentioned above, secondary regional data constitute the main information that supports the evaluated MIAs. This is a cause of concern, particularly when taking into account the coastal zone's changing environmental and climate conditions, as well as its complex structure. Specific in situ measurement and modeling is required to analyze the possible externalities within the regional environmental systems, a thorough analysis of interactions among all indicators

TABLE 7.2 Evaluation of information provided in MIAs

#	TYPE	COMPONENT	SABANCUY 1	2	3	SEYBAPLAYA 4	5
1		Climate	✓	✓	✓	✓	✓
2		Geology	✓	✓	✓	X	✓
3		Geomorphology	✓	X	✓	X	✓
4		Hydrology	✓	✓	✓	✓	✓
5		Water bodies	✓	✓	X	X	✓
6		Groundwater flow	✓	X	X	✓	X
7		Land	✓	✓	X	X	X
8		Water quality	✓	X	X	X	X
9		Precipitation	✓	✓	X	X	X
10	Regional	Bathymetry	X	X	✓	X	X
11		Astronomical tide	✓	✓	✓	X	✓
12		Waves	X	✓	X	X	✓
13		Current	✓	✓	✓	X	✓
14		Wind	✓	✓	X	X	✓
15		Sediment transport	✓	X	X	X	✓
16		Marine flora	✓	✓	✓	X	✓
17		Marine fauna	✓	✓	✓	X	✓
18		Terrestrial flora	✓	✓	✓	✓	✓
19		Terrestrial fauna	✓	✓	✓	✓	✓
20		Population	✓	✓	✓	✓	✓

(continued)

TABLE 7.2, *continued*

#	TYPE	COMPONENT	SABANCUY 1	SABANCUY 2	SABANCUY 3	SEYBAPLAYA 4	SEYBAPLAYA 5
21		Geology	X	✓	X	X	X
22		Geomorphology	X	X	X	X	X
23		Hydrology	X	X	X	X	X
24		Water bodies	X	X	X	X	X
25		Groundwater flow	X	X	X	X	X
26		Land	✓	X	X	X	X
27		Water quality	X	X	X	X	X
28		Precipitation	X	X	X	X	X
29	Specific	Bathymetry	✓	✓	✓	X	✓
30		Astronomical tide	X	X	X	X	X
31		Storm tide	X	X	X	X	X
32		Wind	X	X	X	X	X
33		Waves	X	X	X	X	X
34		Current	X	X	X	X	X
35		Beach profiles	X	X	X	X	X
36		Sedimentation	X	X	X	X	X
37		Simulation of long waves (hydrodynamics)	X	X	X	X	X
38		Wave propagation	X	✓	X	X	X
39		Wave interaction with structures	X	X	X	X	X

that affect the shoreline, and the long-term effects of hard infrastructure development in the coastal region.

Experts that elaborate the study

The Mexican regulatory framework allows anybody to elaborate a MIA, regardless of the complexity of the proposed intervention zone or the project itself.

Only one MIA—for the port of Seybaplaya—was reviewed by an independent research institute. In two cases where the project proponent is a public entity—port authority and Ministry of Transport—the developer itself elaborated the MIA without hiring external specialists for the study.

In addition, SEMARNAT can only reject MIAs when (a) development of the activity or project would violate existing laws or other legal instruments; (b) the activity or project would endanger species or affect already threatened species; or (c) it is based on false information. Under any other circumstances, SEMARNAT is legally mandated to authorize the project, although in doing so, SEMARNAT does have the power to modify the project or condition the approval on the adoption of additional prevention and mitigation measures. The process used to identify such additional measures or project modifications is not regulated. Moreover, the public has no means other than SEMARNAT's resolution to better understand, for example, whether an interdisciplinary team was involved in evaluating the MIAs for complex projects, or whether the effectiveness and efficiency of the additional mitigation measures required by the secretary are well known.

Interinstitutional and public consultation

In compliance with the law, SEMARNAT consulted the project proposals and respective environmental studies with state and municipal authorities. However, no concrete rules or procedures are established by law for these additional consultations. In the end, SEMARNAT has full responsibility for accepting or rejecting the opinions or recommendations provided by any of the consulted agencies. In the Sabancuy region, SEMARNAT consulted the Commission for National Protected Areas for at least one of the MIAs; however, such consultation did not take place for the other project proposals. Additional technical feedback by institutions like the Navy (Secretaría de Marina), the Ministry for Agriculture, Livestock, Rural Development, Fisheries and Food, the National Commission for Biodiversity Knowledge and Use, public universities and investigation centers, among others, could have provided additional technical elements to evaluate the environmental studies underpinning the MIA.

Public consultation is crucial to EIA, particularly given that one of the main goals of EIA is to open up environmental decision making to public scrutiny (Ortolano et al. 1987; Sánchez-Triana and Ortolano 2001). However, SEMARNAT did not organize a public consultation for any of the MIAs evaluated SEMARNAT's decisions were based on the regulatory framework currently in place, under which public consultations are only held under specific circumstances. Specifically, SEMARNAT must decide whether to organize such consultations based on an explicit request by an affected community. In the absence of public consultations, civil society, research institutions, experts, and NGOs can only learn about a project based on the summary published in SEMARNAT's weekly *Environmental Gazette*.

Access to information

In two of five reviewed cases, the proposed project's information that must be publicly available (the environmental impact study and SEMARNAT's final decision on the MIA, including the additional requirements on which the approval is conditioned) was not readily available.

Under these conditions it is difficult for stakeholders and other interested parties to understand fully a project proposal, related environmental studies, and the conditions under which the project must be developed and operated.

1. Conditions and follow-up

Project proponents must propose prevention and mitigation measures for environmental impacts as part of the MIA. The analysis showed that these proposals end up being the conditions under which SEMARNAT approves the MIA, and therefore, the implementation of the project. In a few cases, other consulted public entities proposed additional conditions.

In addition, there is no record on any follow up of these conditions. This would include systematic monitoring of their compliance as a responsibility of the proponent, and field visits by authorities responsible for ensuring compliance with the requirements established by SEMARNAT, particularly the Federal Environmental Attorney (PROFEPA).

2. Reactive vs. proactive environmental management

The proposed projects that were reviewed for this analysis aimed, directly or as a co-benefit, at solving a shoreline problem, mainly coastal erosion.

These cases highlight the role of EIA as an instrument for reactive environmental management, which generates ad hoc responses associated with specific projects. In other words, EIAs are not conducive to addressing large-scale environmental challenges proactively, such as shoreline erosion.

The effectiveness of EIA can be further questioned based on physical observations of the shorelines where interventions were implemented with SEMARNAT's authorization. Specifically, although the reviewed projects included actions to protect the shoreline, satellite images depict a considerable loss of beach cover in both areas, but more clearly in Sabancuy.

ECONOMIC INSTRUMENTS AND INTEGRATED COASTAL ZONE MANAGEMENT[4]

A number of general economic principles form the background philosophy for an economically and environmentally sustainable strategy for natural resource management. These principles are also often cited within the context of ICZM initiatives. The two most often enunciated include the polluter-pays and precautionary principles. The polluter-pays (or user-pays) principle assigns rights that allow internalization of costs that would not normally be incurred by the polluter or user (externalities). The precautionary principle provides a mechanism for dealing with the uncertainty of impacts (O'Riordan and Cameron 1994; Perrings 1991).

A number of mechanisms have been developed and used to promote these principles. At one extreme, they include fines or sanctions that are linked to traditional command-and-control (CAC) regulations. At the other extreme, they include laissez-faire approaches that require consumer advocacy or private litigation to act as incentives for improving environmental management. In between are the more familiar tax-and-subsidy approaches as well as the less familiar mechanisms relying on traded property rights. All of these approaches attempt to internalize environmental costs of natural resource use.

There is no single standardized definition of an incentive-based or market-based instrument (MBI), but the commonly held understanding and the definition employed here is that an MBI must, foremost, attempt to align private costs with social costs to reduce externalities (Panayotou 1994, 1995). Within this definition, the particular strength of an MBI then depends on the degree of *flexibility* that a polluter or resource user has in achieving a given environmental target. A very *weak* MBI essentially dictates through regulation the type of technologies that firms must use, or the targets they must meet. This is the inflexible Command and Control (CAC) approach—which also entails an economic incentive to the extent that failure to comply can result in monetary sanctions. A very *strong* MBI allows market signals rather than explicit directives determine the best way to meet a given standard or goal. EIAs and their associated regulatory structures, sanctions, and fines are typically regarded as part of a CAC approach.

Flexibility is operationalized by equating it to the level of decentralization that occurs in transferring social (or state) decisions to the private (individual) level. A strong MBI decentralizes decision making to a degree that the polluter or resource user has a maximum amount of flexibility to select the production or consumption option that minimizes the social cost of achieving a particular level of environmental quality. Profit- or utility-maximizing behavior in this case also generates a *lowest social cost* outcome for the achievement of a given policy objective.

The framework presented here focuses on the *cost-effectiveness* of *reducing externalities* in defining an MBI. This interpretation provides scope both for internalizing the costs or benefits of any externality while allowing the freedom of choice that will permit users to select an appropriate technology for optimizing environmental quality.

Table 7.3 illustrates the broad spectrum of instruments that might be available, all of which implicitly or explicitly have some incentive effect. They fall across a continuum ranging from very strict command approaches to decentralized

TABLE 7.3 Classification of economic instruments based on flexibility in individual decision–making

MINIMUM FLEXIBILITY		MODERATE FLEXIBILITY		MAXIMUM FLEXIBILITY
CONTROL-ORIENTED		MARKET-ORIENTED		LITIGATION-ORIENTED
GOVERNMENT INVOLVEMENT DECREASING ——>			PRIVATE INITIATIVE INCREASING ——>	
REGULATIONS AND SANCTIONS	CHARGES, TAXES, AND FEES	MARKET CREATION	FINAL DEMAND INTERVENTION	LIABILITY LEGISLATION
GENERAL EXAMPLES				
Standards: Government restricts nature and amount of pollution or resource use for individual polluters or resource users. Compliance is monitored and sanctions imposed (fines, closure, and jail terms) for noncompliance.	Effluent or user charges: Government charges fees to individual polluters or resource users based on amount of pollution or resource use and nature of receiving medium. Fee is high enough to create incentive to reduce impacts. Subsidies: Government provides subsidized inputs to encourage their adoption.	Tradable permits: Government establishes a system of tradable permits for pollution or resource use, auctions or distributes permits, and monitors compliance. Polluters or resource users trade permits at unregulated market prices.	Performance rating: Government supports labeling/performance rating program that requires disclosure of environmental information on the final end-use product. Performance based on adoption of ISO 14000 voluntary guidelines: zero pollution discharge, mitigation plans submitted; pollution prevention technology adopted, reuse policies and waste recycling.	Strict liability legislation: The polluter or resource user is required by law to pay any damages to those affected. Damaged parties collect settlements through litigation and the court system.
Specific examples				
Pollution standards. Licensing of economic activities. Land use restrictions. Zoning and setback requirements. Water use quotas. Construction impact regulations for roads, pipelines, ports, or communications grids. Fines for spills from port or land-based storage facilities. Bans applied to materials deemed unacceptable for solid waste collection services.	Noncompliance pollution charges. Source-based effluent charges to reduce downstream water treatment requirements. Royalties and financial compensation for natural resources exploitation. Performance bonds to ensure construction standards. Subsidies to construct common effluent treatment plans. Tipping fees on solid wastes. User charges for water.	Payment of ecosystem services to forest owners to ensure water protection ecosystem services. Designation of property rights to farmers to improve irrigation water and drainage management. Deposit-refund systems for solid and hazardous wastes. Tradable permits for water abstraction rights, and water and air pollution emissions.	Consumer product labeling (eco-labels) relating to production practices, energy efficiency, and so forth. Supply chain intervention where intermediate buyers insist on installation of effluent treatment plants for upstream product production processes. Education regarding recycling and reuse. Disclosure legislation requiring manufacturers to publish solid, liquid, and toxic waste generation. Blacklist of polluters.	Damages compensation to plaintiff. Liability placed on guilty firm's managers and environmental authorities. Long-term performance bonds posted for potential or uncertain hazards from infrastructure construction. "Zero net impact" requirements for infrastructure projects.

approaches that rely more on market or legal mechanisms. Even traditional CAC regulations, with heavy fines, create a presumed incentive effect because the resource user would be compelled to comply with the regulations to avoid the sanctions.

Goals of incentive-based instruments

In principle, there is a wide range of methods available for attempting to regulate or manage environmental quality. Each of these intends to address a variety of goals. One goal associated with decentralized decision making relates to *cost-effectiveness*. For example, the asymmetry of information often implies that individual agents, private firms, or community associations are more likely than governments to identify the most cost-effective means for achieving a given environmental goal, such as less water withdrawal, less water pollution, or more forest coverage. This forms the basis for the common theoretical result that—if one focuses entirely on private costs—strong forms of MBIs are more cost effective than their weaker counterparts or than CAC approaches (Tietenberg 1990).

Another fundamental goal of most environmental regulatory systems is to *decrease externalities*. Externalities exist where the agent making the production or consumption decision does not bear all of the costs or benefits of this decision. Externalities abound in environmental issues. Disposal of industrial effluent into a waterway may be a low-cost solution to waste disposal for the polluter, but firms and individuals downstream may suffer consequences through higher costs from lost fishery production, higher water treatment costs, lower amenity values (for recreation), or loss of critical drinking water supplies. Most economic incentive structures attempt to transfer some of this cost back to the individual responsible for the decision. A similar situation could exist with environmentally beneficial decisions. For example, a firm that cleans polluted intake water and then discharges clean water after using it in its internal process would be creating a positive externality. In such cases, it could be argued that it is optimal to provide subsidies to such firms in direct proportion to the value of this external benefit.

A third goal that many policymakers have when designing an appropriate economic incentive system is *revenue generation*. There are, however, practical tradeoffs to consider between revenue generation and incentive effects. For example, it would be possible to levy a very high charge that effectively discourages all polluting activity. Abatement levels would be very high in such a case, but no revenue would be generated. Similarly, very low charges would generate little revenue and generate little abatement because there is no incentive for firms to reduce pollution. Typically, revenue is maximized at some intermediate level of abatement. A policy decision must be made relating to how much additional revenue (beyond the maximum) a government is willing to give up to generate higher levels of abatement. The answer to this policy question should be related to the marginal benefits of pollution abatement. However, it is typically more a function of government budgetary realities that regard such taxes as a convenient means for underwriting environmental management efforts.

Types of incentive-based instruments

Regulations, fines, and penalties

Centralized control-oriented approaches relying extensively on regulatory guidelines, permits, or licenses have traditionally been the preferred mechanisms for controlling environmental impacts in urban areas. Although it is technically simple to impose regulations with specific fines for noncompliance, the problems associated with implementing them and achieving compliance are insurmountable for many developing countries.

First, *regulatory drag* can occur when the regulatory approval system, because it is overburdened, unnecessarily holds up critically important investments, and in so doing acts as a drag on economic development prospects. Second, the capacity to implement regulations is often limited because of inadequate human resources, or inadequate supportive infrastructure such as environmental information or monitoring networks. Third, local financing constraints arise because authority for environmental regulations is often delegated to lower (local) levels of government without adequate sources of financing for implementing and monitoring the regulations. Fourth, conflicting standards often prevail where individual ministries or departments have been responsible for setting environmental regulations within their own departments; lack of coordination often leads to conflicting or overlapping regulations. This is often most pronounced for water-related issues, because of the numerous stakeholders involved in water use. Finally, conflict of interest within government programs exists where government agencies are themselves the implementing or investing authority; self-regulation becomes problematic under such circumstances and seldom are there built-in incentives to ensure compliance. This is especially a problem with common infrastructure facilities that typically are a government mandate.

User charges and taxes (or subsidies)

Some of the greatest opportunities for improved environmental management include those arising from appropriate market-oriented instruments. The application of these mechanisms typically has a number of goals. First, incentive effects, which provide economic reasons for polluters or resource users to lower their impacts, are reflected in user charges for typical infrastructure services such as sanitation and water provision. Incentives can also be used to affect intermodal choices: environmental taxes on fuels can discourage private automobile use, and concomitantly reduce demand for complementary public goods such as roads. Second, market-oriented approaches can be used as a recurrent revenue base; this is especially important where local institutions are expected to be financially autonomous, or are required to fund selected regulatory functions. An important variant of the user charge is a *presumptive tax*. The basis of the tax is an effluent charge that is sensitive to a *presumed* level of pollution. A firm is compelled to pay the tax, and no specific monitoring is conducted. If the firm wishes to reduce its tax burden, it must conduct monitoring at its own expense (but still subject to regulatory audit) to demonstrate that its actual pollution loads are less than the presumed loads. Subsidies can also be used as an economic incentive for environmental management. Subsidies on environmentally appropriate behavior are analytically identical to taxes on inappropriate behavior. Such subsidies have been especially common in developing countries for the importation of pollution control technologies or for credit subsidies where the credit is used for environmental investments.

Market creation (permits and deposit-refund)

At a more complex level, market-oriented approaches can include some form of market creation. The most complex system involves tradable permits where user/polluter rights are assigned, according to a desirable total level of use or pollution, and trade achieves compliance. One potential advantage of such systems is that they may reduce bureaucracy and government participation in the process. Such decentralization of decision making is particularly important in high growth economies where regulatory drag might otherwise be a problem. Another potentially important type of market creation involves reform of property rights to confer some form of property right (either individual or collective) in areas of environmental sensitivity. The right holder then has the incentive to manage resource use sustainably, and the legal right to seek compensation from agents that benefit from the resource. Deposit-refund systems are also based on a market created to buy back sources of solid wastes. These have been used extensively to promote recycling. Such schemes are also appropriate for difficult problems such as toxic and hazardous waste management.

Market creation (payment for ecosystem services pes)

The PES approach to environmental protection entails the creation of arrangements where individuals or communities are paid to undertake actions that increase the levels of ecosystem services desired by those who stand to benefit from those services. The Clean Development Mechanism is perhaps the most well-known such arrangement that facilitates the payment by the global community for carbon emission reductions, to those providing the emission-reduction ecosystem service. PES policies are a growing trend because they offer a direct and possibly poverty-alleviating method for achieving environmental objectives. However, transaction costs of implementation, monitoring and enforcement can be high if the large number of agents is high such as when there are many individual landowners whose collective action threatens certain ecosystem services.

Final demand intervention (eco-labeling, disclosure requirements, or environmental awareness)

Eco-labeling to promote environmentally sound production and packaging is a relatively passive form of intervention; it decentralizes decision making to the final consumer. A more aggressive form involves promulgating disclosure requirements: firms are required to publish precisely what they pollute. There are no sanctions attached to such disclosure but consumers are then given the choice of how to deal with the products of particular firms. Another example of education and awareness building, targeted to industries, is the UNIDO waste minimization program that assists in identifying appropriate technologies for specific plant and industry types. The programs typically improve energy and material efficiency for plants, while at the same time reducing waste generation. All such interventions can effectively reduce urban infrastructure requirements, improve environmental quality, and have important spin-offs in other social sectors. Their major disadvantage is that they typically require some form of subsidy.

Final demand intervention (supply-chain management)

Related to eco-labeling, firms are increasingly sensitive about the environmental and social context in which their suppliers operate. In such cases, firms downstream in the supply chain intervene in the upstream production processes of their intermediate products by insisting that certain environmental protection activities are undertaken in during production. These types of interventions have resulted in upstream firms installing pollution control equipment to satisfy their buyers' sourcing criteria.

Liability legislation

Litigation-oriented approaches to environmental management require only that legislation be in place that confers relatively straightforward rights and obligations to resource users. These approaches form a legal umbrella for court cases, which then consider the nature and extent of environmental damages on a case-by-case basis. Most of these approaches are relatively new, and have seen very limited application in developing countries (quite often because legal systems are themselves weak in such countries). Even in industrial countries, they are hampered by the analytical difficulties of establishing cause and effect, or of ascribing blame or negligence.

One significant objection to using litigation-oriented mechanisms is neither environmental nor economic: it is social. Because such systems assume that all have equal access to the courts, the mechanisms often discriminate against the poor and others with limited access to legal recourse.

Lessons and implications for integrated coastal zone management

In each of the cases considered, there is usually both an incentive element as well as a control element. Simply stated, there is no getting around the classic "carrot and stick." Experience with these types of mechanisms around the world has shown that they have different advantages and disadvantages, and that depending on the goals of the government, some mechanisms are better than others are. The following general conclusions can be drawn from this experience:

- Systems based solely on control-oriented approaches impose high private costs and often are not enforceable given existing institutional capacity. Mexico's current EIA system also exhibits these characteristics
- Litigation-oriented approaches require the development of a strong legal system to which all members of society have equal access
- Market-oriented instruments allow polluters and resource users to find their own best mix of controls or responses, and therefore result in lower private costs than other approaches
- Local authorities and strong institutional support play an important role in the success of market-oriented mechanisms.

In the context of ICZM, the complexity of problems and issues does not always lend itself to a single approach. Indeed, even CAC systems benefit from complementary market-based approaches, legal relief through publicly accessible regulatory and court processes, and voluntary mechanisms by industries that meet local social and environmental goals while also contributing to cost-effective operations. An appropriate way forward for EIA reforms is to identify and implement such complementary market-based approaches.

SUMMARY

Mexico's legal framework and practice are not particularly suited for coastal management. Arguably, from its conception, EIA was not meant to be the predominant environmental management tool, but to complement other legal, economic, and administrative instruments by opening up environmental authorities' decision making to public scrutiny, particularly in relation to projects likely to cause significant environmental impacts. However, in Mexico, as in other countries, EIA has become the main environmental management tool and is often the only instrument used to address complex environmental problems, as exemplified by coastal zone management in Campeche.

In the reviewed cases, EIA practice had a number of limitations. These include preparation of environmental impact studies based on incomplete data, insufficient participation from independent experts in the preparation and evaluation of the MIA, weak public participation, absence of formal criteria to evaluate the MIA, and weak enforcement and follow-up to ensure that the project developer complies with all the requirements that SEMARNAT established during the EIA process.

The laws and regulations include a large number of activities for which an EIA must be undertaken. SEMARNAT is required to approve all MIAs, unless they fall under the specific circumstances mentioned above. As a result, SEMARNAT receives a very large number of MIAs every year, which it has to evaluate under tight deadlines. As a rough comparison, in Mexico an average of 2,786 projects per year were submitted to the EIA process between 2008 and 2012, compared with an average of 463 projects per year in the United States.[5] The resources and time that SEMARNAT has available for each of these projects is limited, curtailing opportunities to engage other agencies, external specialists, or the public. Lack of resources is also a constraint to conduct field visits for supervision and enforcement.

As in Mexico, most countries in Latin America use lists to determine which projects or activities are subject to an EIA (Sánchez-Triana and Enriquez, 2007). The existence of such lists is supposed to reduce discretionary decision making. However, they generate a different problem: the rigidity of the lists limits their ability to filter out the actions that would not generate significant environmental effects. Lists are also used to determine whether a regional or a specific MIA should be prepared. In the specific case of coastal areas, only large aquaculture projects would call for a regional MIA. Other cases that would trigger the preparation of a regional MIA include projects with potential synergistic, cumulative, or residual impacts on ecosystems. However, there is a need for methodologies, guidelines, and regulations to guide effective cumulative and synergistic impact assessments. Arguably, many projects in coastal areas would likely have cumulative or synergistic impacts. However, as the reviewed cases show, the EIA for projects in the coast of Campeche did not need to address these types of impacts.

EIA's potential contributions to ICZM are also limited because of insufficient involvement of independent experts, which is not required under the regulatory framework in place. In addition, project developers are responsible for hiring the consultant who prepares the EIA, resulting in a clear conflict of interests. Developers' main interests are meeting the bare minimum legal requirements and overcoming any potential objections to the project. Consultants thus have incentives to focus on these objectives, rather than on conducting rigorous environmental studies.

Public participation can add value to the EIA process by making visible the problems, constraints, opportunities, and challenges that tended to be hidden by limited screening, scoping, and environmental impact studies' preparation stages. However, public hearings are often resource-intensive and, if not properly organized, can easily turn into a community's opportunity to voice demands for issues with little or no relationship to the project's environmental impacts.

Clearly regulating the public hearings process, as well as complying with other provisions aiming to facilitate public participation, such as ensuring that the relevant information is publicly available, could strengthen EIA practice in Mexico.

One of the fundamental contributions of EIA is the identification of mitigation measures that can be implemented to avoid, minimize, or offset the negative effects associated with the proposed project. For this reason, the EIA process includes a follow-up mechanism that would ideally help authorities to ensure that the conditions for approval are fulfilled, to monitor whether the action's environmental impacts are similar to those predicted by the environmental impact study, to assess whether the selected mitigation measures are effective, and to generate information to improve other EIAs.

In Mexico, as in other countries, environmental authorities rarely monitor the action's impacts after the corresponding license or permit has been issued, mainly due to lack of resources (Sánchez-Triana and Enriquez 2007). Exploring mechanisms to increase the resources available to environmental agencies, such as including the cost of supervision in the fees paid by developers, is therefore crucial to improve EIA's effectiveness.

NOTES

1. The case studies were carried out by Dr. Gregorio Posada under the supervision of Ernesto Sánchez-Triana and Katharina Siegmann.
2. For a detailed comparison of EIA systems in Latin America, see Ruth Tiffer-Sotomayor, Ernesto Sánchez-Triana, Ana Luisa Gomes Lima, Rosario Navarro, Santiago Enriquez, Katharina Siegmann, and Pilar Clemente Fernández. 2014. *Comparative Matrix: EIA Framework in Latin America*. Washington, DC: World Bank. http://conferences.iaia.org/2015/Final-Papers/Tiffer,%20R%20et%20al.%202015-Poster-%20LAC-%20EIA%20Legal%20Framework-final-l.pdf.
3. General Law of Ecological Equilibrium and Environmental Protection, 1998, amended by DOF 09-01-2015; Regulations of the General Law of Ecological Equilibrium for Environmental Impact Assessment, 2000, amended by DOF 31-10-2014 LEEGEPA.
4. Based on Ruitenbeek 2015. Refer also to Huber et al. 1998.
5. Data for Mexico are from http://www.cmic.org/comisiones/sectoriales/turismo/noticias_principales/greenexpo/Env%C3%ADro%20Pro/Miercoles/Impacto%20Amb.%20y%20Manejo%20BPCs/env252-MenCAlfonsoFlores.pdf. Data for the United States are from http://www.gao.gov/assets/670/662543.pdf.

REFERENCES

O'Riordan, T., and J. Cameron, eds. 1994. *Interpreting the Precautionary Principle*. London: Earthscan.

Ortolano, L., B. Jenkins, and R. Abracosa. 1987. "Speculations on When and Why EIA Is Effective." *Environmental Impact Assessment Review* 7 (4): 285–92.

Panayotou, T. 1994. *Economic Instruments for Environmental Management and Sustainable Development*. Harvard Institute for International Development. Cambridge, MA: Harvard University.

———. 1995. "Market-Based Instruments in Environmental Management: Experiences and Perspectives." Developing Countries: Proceedings of the International Conference, Berlin, June 5–9, 1994.

Perrings, C. 1991. "Reserved Rationality and the Precautionary Principle: Technological Change, Time and Uncertainty in Environmental Decision-Making." In *Ecological Economics: The*

Science and Management of Sustainability, 153–66, edited by R. Costanza. New York, NY: Columbia University Press.

Sánchez-Triana, E., and S. Enriquez. 2007. *A Comparative Analysis of Environmental Impact Assessment Systems in Latin American. Draft version*. A World Bank Study. Washington, DC: World Bank. http://www.ifc.org/wps/wcm/connect/c688c7004c08ac00ae87be 79803d5464/2_EIA+in+LAC+IAIA+Seoul.pdf?MOD=AJPERES.

Sánchez-Triana, E., and L. Ortolano. 2001. "Organizational Learning and Environmental Impact Assessment at Colombia's Cauca Valley Corporation." *Environmental Impact Assessment Review* 21 (3): 223–39.

Tietenberg, T. H. 1990." Economic Instruments for Environmental Regulation." *Oxford Review of Economic Policy* 6 (1): 17–33.

8 Conclusions

ERNESTO SÁNCHEZ-TRIANA, JACK RUITENBEEK, AND SANTIAGO ENRIQUEZ

Approximately 4.1 million people live in the three coastal states of the Yucatán Peninsula: Quintana Roo, Yucatán, and Campeche. Some 30 municipalities from these states are in a coastal territory of almost 2,000 kilometers, spanning the oil fields of the Gulf of Mexico to the world-renowned beaches of Cancún and Cozumel, just north of the second largest barrier reef in the world. The peninsula's natural assets also include some of the nation's most notable cultural assets—Mayan temples including Chichén Itzá, Ek Balám, Uxmal, and Dzibilchaltún.

With poverty far from eliminated, and economic development opportunities beckoning in agriculture, manufacturing and hydrocarbon development, the region is under growing risks to environmental hazards. Oil spills, hurricanes, coral bleaching, extreme flooding and erosion have all been experienced in this region over the past decade. The analytical work presented in this report indicates that environmental health risks also impose substantial economic costs on the region and curtail the local population's opportunities for economic advancement. The main environmental health risks in the peninsula result in more than 1,000 premature deaths every year and in more than 9.36 million days lost to illnesses. In addition to pain and suffering, these risks also generate substantial economic losses, representing 2.2–3.3 percent of GRI.

In terms of health impacts in the peninsula, household air pollution is the most severe problem, followed by outdoor air pollution; these two types of air pollution are responsible for around 80 percent of deaths associated with an environmental health risk. Adult lead (Pb) exposure and inadequate water, sanitation and hygiene caused 13 percent and 7 percent of these deaths, respectively. From an economic standpoint, lead exposure is the cause of 48 percent of the cost of environmental degradation, mostly because it results in impaired intelligence in children and a consequent reduction in lifetime earnings. About 26 percent of the cost is from household air pollution, 16 percent is from outdoor air pollution, and 10 percent of the cost is from inadequate water, sanitation and hygiene.

This report has also presented estimates of the economic impacts of natural disasters under climate change. Available data show upward trends in terms of both the frequency and severity of natural resources in the Yucatán Peninsula, particularly since 1985. These trends are expected to continue in the future. If the peninsula's economy were to grow 2–3 percent annually, the annual mean economic cost of extreme weather events (ordinary events) would be about 0.4 percent of gross domestic product (GDP). This figure is about double the annual cost of natural disasters for Mexico as a whole. However, in the 95th percentile (when the damages would be highest) this cost could reach 1.4–1.5 percent of GDP in 2020 and 1.6–2.3 percent of GDP in 2050 (Government of Yucatán 2012). These figures underscore the urgency of reducing vulnerability through appropriate emergency preparedness, risk mitigation, and integrated coastal zone management (ICZM) efforts. Adaptation interventions in the Yucatán Peninsula should consider both relatively infrequent, but catastrophic events, and events with less severe impacts, but that occur frequently.

The three states in the Yucatán Peninsula share a common geography and to a certain extent, development challenges such as climate change. While there are important socioeconomic differences between the states, coastal ecosystems provide fundamental ecosystem services for all of them, including protection from extreme weather events and resources that underpin their economic activities. However, as discussed in this report, coastal ecosystems face a number of challenges, including severe erosion and impacts from unplanned urban expansion, infrastructure development, and significant pollution. These challenges are likely to be exacerbated because of climate change, particularly if current environmental degradation trends continue, thereby eroding the resilience of natural ecosystems.

A major challenge to confront these problems is the need to strengthen the institutional framework. In Mexico, coastal management is undertaken largely through three policy instruments: (a) Environmental Impact Assessment, (b) the creation of Marine Protected Zones, and (c) ecological zoning. However, these instruments are also insufficient to tackle the coastal area's priority issues, including sea level rise and coastal erosion.

The analytical work presented in this report included the preparation of case studies to better understand the role of environmental impact assessment (EIA) in supporting management of coastal zones. In the reviewed cases, EIA practice had a number of potential constraints. These included the need to enforce follow-up to ensure that the project developer complies with all the requirements that SEMARNAT established during the EIA process.

Arguably, part of the problem is that EIA has become the predominant environmental management tool in Mexico. An average of 2,786 projects per year was submitted to the EIA process in Mexico between 2008 and 2012.[1] Because of this extensive use of EIA, SEMARNAT establishes ad hoc requirements for each authorized project. Given that EIA is aimed at opening up environmental authorities' decision making to public scrutiny—particularly in relation to projects likely to cause significant environmental impacts—it is necessary to further evaluate the EIA process's effectiveness and efficiency.

The main ecological planning instruments in Mexico are Territorial Environmental Land Use Programs (POEGTs) and Urban Development Plans (PDUs). Both POEGTs and PDUs are sometimes hampered by a lack of technical and institutional capacity within local and municipal governments for overseeing the complex tasks involved in assessing environmental needs, setting priorities, and building consensus among stakeholders (Hardoy et al. 2014; Creel 2005). There is also a certain level of unwieldiness to the creation of a POEGT. To date, there have been no rigorous attempts to evaluate the effectiveness and efficiency of the preparation and enforcement of POEGTs, most of which lack an appropriate monitoring and evaluation framework (INE 2012).

In the Yucatán Peninsula, there are three regional and 10 municipal POEGTs.[2] However, some large areas are yet to be covered by a POEGT. Specifically, Campeche's coastal zone lacks a regional POEGT, and in Quintana Roo, only the Sian Ka'an region is covered by a regional POEGT. Within the Yucatán Peninsula, only Yucatán's coast is entirely covered by a regional program. In fact, most of Mexico's coastal zones lack a POEGT. These plans, however, are a valuable consensus-making tool and provide one of the best ways of formalizing the agreements that need to be made if various municipalities, states, and ministries are going to work together.

An effective approach to address coastal management issues would be to develop a Shoreline Management Plan (SMP), setting out how the coast should best be managed in the future. The development of a sediment budget is a critical stage in the development of the conceptual model for the plan. A major obstacle that needs to be overcome to establish this sediment budget is the lack of information that would facilitate building up a composite map of sediment sources, sinks, stores and pathways. Since predicting future coastal change is the end product of the study, the changes in wave or tidal energy, the sources and sinks for sediment, and human inhibition of sediment movement all contribute to coastal morphological change and form the basis for the conceptual model. Thus, the conceptual modeling stage of the SMP must depend on the collation of an adequate database. The governments of the Yucatán Peninsula would benefit from establishing an institutional framework that would allow collection of the required primary and secondary data.

Another priority challenge for the Yucatán Peninsula's coastal areas is the lack of sustainability of the tourism model that has driven economic growth, particularly in Quintana Roo. This represents an important case of an economy whose development has been led by the expansion of the tourist industry organized around the traditional model of the tourist enclave and beach resort concentration. Deteriorating environmental conditions and changing international trends combined with climate change threats have made this tradition obsolete as a model of industrial organization, and increasingly unreliable as an engine of sustainable development. Moreover, the model has excluded local populations, particularly indigenous households, from its economic benefits.

Because of its riches in terms of natural beauty, cultural heritage and human potential, Quintana Roo appears particularly apt to accept the challenge of converting its economy toward the new type of tourism, based on lower scale development, devoted to the ecological and cultural aspects of the visitors' experience, higher social and economic inclusion, and a more integrated economic structure. The SAM developed as part of the analytical work helped to explore and test these hypotheses using available statistics, the results of a field survey of a sample of international and national tourists, and a field survey of and of local households.

The analysis conducted seems to corroborate the hypothesis that Quintana Roo can develop its economy at a faster pace and with a more balanced growth by differentiating its development model. This differentiation can be achieved by (a) rebalancing the spatial pattern of development through land use planning and regulation, with special attention to controlling urban sprawl and conserving the coastal ecosystem; (b) promoting small-scale development of the tourism supply chain more widely, based on local entrepreneurship and small and specialized operators; (c) investing in environmental and biodiversity conservation; (d) investing in tourism development through basic infrastructure (water, sanitation, and feeder roads) and nonbasic infrastructure (access and maintenance of archaeological sites, parks, and museums), not only in proximity to the beaches and seafronts, but also in the forest and wetland areas; and (v) encouraging the indigenous population's involvement in the various segments of the tourism supply chain, including agriculture, transportation, lodging, and tourism operations.

NEXT STEPS

This report has highlighted the need to fill scientific knowledge gaps and to develop a strong knowledge base that can inform decision making and lead to an integrated coastal zone management, resulting in enhanced environmental, economic, and social resilience in the Yucatán Peninsula. In addition, this report's findings provide compelling arguments to develop specific interventions to tackle the obstacles to environmentally healthy, inclusive, and resilient growth faced by the Yucatán Peninsula.

A major obstacle to confront the peninsula's development challenges is the lack of a formal priority setting mechanism and an adequate institutional framework to align available resources with the most pressing environmental challenges. Using rigorous priority-setting tools, such as the cost of environmental degradation study presented in this report, is an important step to fill this gap. Once environmental priorities have been set, institutional resources should be aligned to address them, and if needed, policies or regulations should be adopted or reformed to efficiently and effectively tackle the issues that are causing the most severe damages. Monitoring and evaluation systems should also be strengthened to assess the extent to which the objectives of environmental priorities are being met. Accumulation of data, results, and experiences in policy design and implementation should be integrated into the M&E systems to support continuous social learning that underpins further policy improvements.

As explained in chapter 3, the existing regulatory toolkit is inadequate to promote ICZM in the Yucatán Peninsula. SMPs are a proven approach to achieve long-term sustainability of coastal risk management for a specific stretch of coast. Developing an SMP includes five main tasks: (a) defining sediment cells as the basic unit for coastal zone management, (b) collating a coastal database designed to support the science within the SMP, (c) developing conceptual (or behavioral) models for each sediment cell, (d) evaluating societal demands on the coast, and (e) reconciling scientific and societal demands within the SMP framework.

To conduct these tasks, the next steps should focus on the collection, storage, and retrieval of coastal data that can be used to develop the conceptual models of the coast. Data should be acquired from both primary and secondary sources. The advantage of using secondary data is that secondary data can reduce both costs and time. However, in many cases secondary data sources are either lacking or inadequate.

The existing database for the Yucatán Peninsula is not considered adequate to support any detailed shoreline management. What limited data is available is focused on local issues at scales significantly smaller than those of the sediment cells outlined in chapter 3. This means that management tends to rely on reducing local impacts, rather than seeking general causes of coastal problems. The lack of any data on waves, tides, currents, bathymetry, shoreline topography, and the minimal data on sea level rise must be seen as a major impediment to effective shoreline management. Specific actions are needed to lay the foundations for an information system that can integrate existing and new data to help fill these data gaps.

Given the significant impacts caused by environmental degradation in the Yucatán Peninsula, as explained in chapter 5, the environmental information system should also integrate data that will underpin the development of effective and efficient interventions to tackle environmental health risks. Indoor and outdoor air pollution causes the most significant health impacts. Therefore, the monitoring system should prioritize monitoring of emissions, concentrations and exposure levels to fine particulate matter in outdoor and indoor environments. Initial efforts could focus on monitoring PM2.5, and gradually expand its capacity to monitor PM1.0 as well. The monitoring system should also include a source and composition inventory of the source structure of both primary and secondary PM in order to guide future air quality management planning and interventions. The monitoring system could also include black carbon emissions, a pollutant linked to PM, with known effects on the climate and on human health.

It is also critical to improve the knowledge base on lead exposure, because it is the environmental health risk causing the most-significant economic losses in the Yucatán Peninsula. Although blood lead levels have been decreasing over time, efforts should be made to identify and control lead exposure in *hotspots*. In addition, in light of recent evidence of the severity of impacts of lead in children, measurement studies should be undertaken to confirm blood lead levels among children, map geographic pockets of high blood lead levels, and identify and control sources of lead exposure.

In addition to building the information system mentioned above, steps to address the peninsula's sustainability challenges would include the preparation of pre-feasibility, feasibility, and design studies for specific interventions on coastal management, pollution control, environmental health, and management of natural ecosystems through strengthened management of natural protected areas and Reduced Emissions from Deforestation and Degradation (REDD+). These studies would help to identify the most efficient and effective alternatives to tackle the regional environmental priorities presented in this report.

TABLE 8.1 Summary of recommendations

CATEGORY	ACTIONS	TIME FRAME
Pilot projects and interventions	• Develop pilot projects to control beach erosion in priority sites, using existing information	Short term
	• Replicate pilot projects throughout the peninsula's coastal areas	Medium term
	• Develop shoreline management plans	Medium term
Technical assistance	• Develop pre-feasibility, feasibility, and engineering design and detail studies for coastal erosion, pollution control, and environmental health risk interventions	Short term
Institutional strengthening	• Establish the leadership and institutional arrangements and capacities to set priorities in environmental policy design and implementation	Short term
	• Align environmental expenditure with priorities	Medium term
	• Enhance capacity of environmental agencies on technical, financial, and managerial issues	Medium term
	• Set horizontal and vertical coordination incentives and quantifiable goals	Medium term
	• Strengthen institutional learning and build the necessary feedback loops to mainstream improvements and change	Medium term
Monitoring, evaluation, research, and development	• Generate, collect, and analyze information on waves, tides, currents, bathymetry, shoreline topography, and sea level rise	Short term
	• Establish monitoring networks to monitor atmospheric air pollution in large urban areas, focusing on PM2.5	Short term
	• Establish monitoring networks to monitor indoor air pollution in rural households, focusing on PM2.5	Short term
	• Conduct studies to confirm blood lead levels among children, map geographic pockets of high blood lead levels, and identify and control sources of lead exposure	Short term
	• Expand the information system to include additional data, including water quality, soil quality, and waste management	Medium term

In addition, as explained in chapter 4, two types of economic losses are associated with the extreme weather events affecting the Yucatán Peninsula: (a) relatively modest losses caused by low-intensity, but frequently occurring natural hazards; and (b) high losses caused by catastrophic events that occur more rarely. Studies should be prepared to assess the adaptation interventions that could be implemented to reduce vulnerability to both kinds of economic losses, recognizing that the benefits and costs of interventions to address the impacts of low intensity events can be quantified with more certainty than those focusing on catastrophic events.

The matrix in table 8.1 summarizes this report's recommendations to help overcome the main obstacles to green and inclusive growth faced by the Yucatán Peninsula.

NOTES

1. http://www.cmic.org/comisiones/sectoriales/turismo/noticias_principales/greenexpo/Env%C3%ADro%20Pro/Miercoles/Impacto%20Amb.%20y%20Manejo%20BPCs/env252-MenCAlfonsoFlores.pdf.
2. http://www.semarnat.gob.mx/sites/default/files/documentos/ordenamiento/decretados_20150617.jpg.

REFERENCES

Creel, J. E. 2005. "Protected Areas and Coastal and Ocean Management in Mexico." *Ocean & Coastal Management* 48 (11): 1016–46.

Gobierno de Yucatán. 2012. *Análisis de la vulnerabilidad actual y futura ante los efectos del cambio climático*. Programa Especial de Acción ante el Cambio Climático del Estado de Yucatán. Mérida, Yucatán.

Hardoy, J., I. Hernández, J. A. Pacheco, and G. Sierra. 2014. "Institutionalizing Climate Change Adaptation at Municipal and State Level in Chetumal and Quintana Roo, Mexico." *Environment and Urbanization* 26 (1): 69–85. doi: 10.1177/0956247813519053.

INE (Instituto Nacional de Ecología). 2012. *10 Propuestas de mejora inmediata para el Ordenamiento Ecológico Territorial* (10 Proposals for Immediate Improvement for Territorial Ecological Planning). http://www.semarnat.gob.mx/sites/default/files/documentos/ordenamiento/10propuestas_mejora_oet_inecc.pdf.

www.ingramcontent.com/pod-product-compliance
Lightning Source LLC
Chambersburg PA
CBHW080426270326
41929CB00018B/3171